Critical Guides to French Texts

8 Duras: Moderato cantabile

Critical Guides to French Texts

EDITED BY ROGER LITTLE, WOLFGANG VAN EMDEN,
DAVID WILLIAMS

MARGUERITE DURAS

Moderato cantabile

David Coward

Senior Lecturer in French
University of Leeds

Grant & Cutler Ltd
1981

© Grant & Cutler Ltd
   1981
ISBN 0 7293 0107 9

I.S.B.N. 84-499-4882-7

DEPÓSITO LEGAL: V. 1.894 - 1981

Printed in Spain by
Artes Gráficas Soler, S. A. - Olivereta, 28 - Valencia (18)
for
GRANT AND CUTLER LTD
11 BUCKINGHAM STREET, LONDON, W.C.2.

Contents

Note

Page references in the text are to the edition in the Collection 10/18, Paris: Union Générale d'Editions, first published in that form in 1962, followed by the edition in the Collection Double, Paris: Les Editions de Minuit, 1980, thus: (p. 42; 31).

Biographical Note

MARGUERITE Duras was born in 1914 at Gia-Dinh in Indo-China, the second of the three children of Henri and Marie Donnadieu, both teachers, who had arrived from France in about 1910. Marguerite's father died in 1918 and the family was reduced almost to poverty. However, her mother, through hard work and determination, educated her three children, sending her to school at Saigon and later to Paris where Mme Duras began reading mathematics but finally emerged with a degree in law. In 1935, she entered the French civil service and worked in the Colonial Office until she resigned in 1941 to become a writer. Her first novel, completed by 1938, the year of her marriage, was rejected by seven publishers before it appeared in 1943 under the nom-de-plume of Duras, which is the name of the Gascon village where she had lived for a brief period in her teens. By this time, Mme Duras had a foot in Parisian literary and existentialist circles and was a member of the French Communist Party from which she was expelled in 1950. During the fifties and sixties, her highly original novels led her to be linked with the school of 'new realism', but it was her script for Alain Resnais's film, *Hiroshima mon amour,* which made her name internationally known. Always ready to involve herself in current affairs — the Algerian War, the Revolution of May 1968 and, recently, the feminist move-ment — Mme Duras has turned her attention increasingly towards politics and the cinema. Since 1971, she has abandoned the novel and has made a dozen enigmatic, low-budget films. Totally committed to her work which she sees as a great politico-aesthetic adventure, Marguerite Duras is one of the most original and controversial figures on the contemporary French literary scene.

Biographical Note

1

Marguerite Duras and 'New Realism'

IN *The Republic,* Plato asks us to consider two types of reality, the one superficial and immediate, the other durable but elusive. We perceive the first with our senses, which interpret the exterior of things; the second is more difficult to grasp, for it lies beneath the surface and beyond the reach of the senses. He invites us to imagine that we live in a cave; that we are so placed that we can see only the wall that is furthest away from its mouth; that the light at the entrance is at our back. Between us and the light is a path along which other people and things come and go: the shadows they cast are projected over our heads onto the rocky cave wall. What we see is the distorted representation of the shadow of things, and this we are likely to call reality. But true reality — that is, those movements and objects which project the shadows — is behind us not before us, light not shadow, proportion not deformity, authenticity not illusion. Reality is an essence of truth which we can grasp only with great difficulty.

For more than two thousand years, the myth of the cave has lain at the heart of the western philosophical tradition. It assumed that existence is a cipher for a deeper reality, a final and absolute essence of things which it was the thinker's duty to isolate and interpret. But a century or so ago, certain philosophers began to believe that, though great efforts had been made to penetrate the phenomena of existence, man seemed no nearer than Plato to that essence of truth. Perhaps there was no essence to be discovered. Perhaps existence itself is the final reality. Instead of peering through a glass darkly, the philosopher had only to look at the world about him.

One of the major avenues explored in the last hundred years by modern — and especially continental — philosophers, has centred upon this important switch in objectives. But what began as a philosophical problem quickly slipped into the literary and artistic consciousness of the twentieth century. If Picasso painted strange shapes and blue people, it was an invitation to the observer to consider the significance of forms and appearance. In a similar vein, Mallarmé's preoccupation with symbols required the reader to grapple with surfaces and make sense of them rather than to interpret allegories in search of the traditional final abstractions. In other words, concern with existential matters undermined the very objectives of the classical mind which sought to bring order out of chaos and reduce the phenomena of the world to acceptable, logical patterns. The advanced artistic consciousness of our century has been directed at existence itself, which is not to be explained in terms either of reason or of faith. The role of the artist has been therefore to teach us to see what we look at.

His business is to start from what is and no longer to annotate it in the light of a philosophical or theological absolute, for there is no final authority. Experience is an experiment and he attempts to understand, not to explain. The reality which is perceived by the avant-garde artist is qualitatively the same as that perceived by his predecessors. But his expectations are both lower and higher. Lower, because he no longer believes that he will find accommodations which are true for all places and in all times. Higher, because he himself assumes responsibility for his quest and no longer resorts to external modes of authority and the commonly accepted, essentialist delusions. His apprehension of reality is probably no more acute than that of earlier masters. But his need to get the most out of himself is far greater, for he knows that unless he is able to come to terms with what is, nobody and no ideology will do it for him.

Of course, not all twentieth century artists and writers have been equally concerned by the shift from 'essence' to 'existence'. Not all have jettisoned God or other forms of authority, such as Marxism. Nor it is true that all nations have responded to the challenge with the same enthusiasm. The traditional view of experience reduced to a formal synthesis underwritten

by an external hypothesis still predominates — from E. M.
Forster's 'Only connect' and its assumption of humanist
values, to Bernanos's attempt to revive a truly Christian
consciousness or, more recently, to feminist novels which
spring from a body of ideology which concerns the position
of women in society. Yet throughout Europe, efforts have been
made to push back the proper frontiers of art. Joyce expanded
a single day into a long journey which he described as an
odyssey. Kafka plunged into the self and its attempts to come
to grips with reality. Existentialist writers in France rejected
all hypotheses except the primordiality of existence and thence
gravitated towards various attitudes which they rarely dignified
with the name of solutions. Camus recommended 'communion'
and Sartre surrendered to a political apprehension of phenomena which may be equated with a certain kind of natural
justice.

Many of the efforts to widen the scope of art have been
greeted with derision, and accusations of obscurantism are not
uncommon. Nowhere has the attempt to set literary expression
in a non-essentialist framework been more marked than in
France, the home of the 'new novel'. If this 'new novel', it is
argued, is really to serve a useful purpose in opening minds
to the errors of essentialist prejudice, then it is odd that it
has not striven to reach a wider audience. It seems to take
pride in being 'difficult' and its inaccessibility is carried like a
banner which declares the independence of the artist and his
abnegation of duty to his reader who must work even harder
than the writer if the message is to be understood. Art is in
danger of losing touch with common humanity and, it is said,
is on the point of turning into a minority cult for highly
trained (though not necessarily well educated) élites.

It is not necessary to evoke theories of populist or even
popular literature to see the point of such criticisms. New
techniques of expression offer a challenge which those who
lack specialised skills or knowledge (of form or of linguistic
and philosophical principles) may find difficult to meet. And
the increasingly abstract concerns of the artist may seem
perverse and his attitudes tentative and elusive. But if the

pursuit of novelty for its own sake is of limited value, the detection of 'mere' novelty is never easy. The artist has both a right and a duty to move his art forward, for it is unthinkable that he should continue to say the same things in the same ways. Once we grant this essential freedom to the artist, we must trust to his wisdom and accept what he offers as worthy of the most serious attention. Impressionist painters were ridiculed for turning their backs on pure Academic line and form — but only until the public eye became attuned to accept and admire their hazy descriptions in which precise details were less important than mood or the overall 'impression'. The test of art is always survival. Until such time as literary history delivers its judgment on the 'New Novel', the new novelists need to be approached with, at the very least, an open mind.

It is already widely accepted, for instance, that the novel, which has provided many generations of readers with invaluable insights into the springs of human conduct, has itself generated misapprehensions of reality. A Balzac novel unfolds slowly, isolating relevant factors which then move into a specific conjuction which in turn precipitates a crisis which is resolved. It satisfies our taste for stories and ties up loose ends, but leaves the mistaken idea that neat patterns are part of life itself — even though our experience would suggest rather that beginnings are not resolved by crises which are, in fact, relatively rare. On the contrary, it would seem that life is a succession of middles, a tangle of loose ends: it is a viewpoint which fits ill with our expectation that stories must end and end in such a way that some sort of idea emerges from the drama we have observed. In *Jacques le fataliste* (1773), Diderot openly discussed the progress of his tale with his reader, teased him by withholding dramatic turns of events and offered three possible endings any of which 'might have' happened. It is an early statement of the dissatisfaction with the novel-as-story and an instruction in what the business of the novelist should be.

Many post-war novelists, building upon earlier experiments, have rejected the 'realistic' tradition of fiction for its denial of reality. The omniscient narrator, like Balzac or Flaubert, is guilty of directing our attention not to what is but to what he needs us to see. By providing richly observed psychological portraits, he fixes character in a literary solution (as scientific specimens are fixed in a bottle) so as to explain behaviour, root it in truth and capture an essence. But what he does in fact is to construct an environment which is limited by his own personality, release a rat and watch it run. Thus the traditional novel imposes limits upon experience by obtaining our agreement to a particular view of reality which states that actions are explained by circumstances, that one event will lead to another in a climactic scale, that situations resolve themselves completely and that every story tells a tale. The traditional novelist plays both upon our need for explanations and our acquired knowledge of the semiology of fiction. By his tone of voice we know what to expect and we respond accordingly because we recognise the signals. In other words, the reader of traditional novels is not shown reality but only what he is prepared — and has been prepared — to see.

The 'New Novelists' discard the tendentiousness of the traditional fiction for these and other reasons. They seek to break fresh ground and to present reality unobstructed by the conventional screens. Omniscience in the narrator gives way to a plain and unemotional objectivism. Locations are no longer described as a 'setting' but are evoked with the barest hints because, after all, what happens must happen somewhere. 'Story' is replaced by an expanded situation which neither begins nor ends and the psychology of 'characters' is replaced by reactions to specific stimuli. Robbe-Grillet's *La Jalousie* dwells on the suspicions of a narrator/camera who recasts the same small details with variations until they begin to lead to a conclusion at which point the book ends: there is no 'drama', save in the emerging clarity of a disembodied perception of consciousness. If this sounds 'difficult', it is, for to read *La Jalousie* we must put aside our expectations that the narrator will translate his doubts into decisive, dramatic action. The 'New Realists' do not compromise their aims by pandering to their audience: we must go with them or we must stay behind. They take us into confused time-zones, through elliptical or geometrical structures and towards a world of looking and seeing in which dialogue no longer records conversations but provides echoes of a tentative inner monologue. Aspects only of a situation may be revealed and it is for the reader to supply what is missing: for only then will the whole become incompletely, disturbingly real. Gide's term, *la mise en abyme,* has frequently been used to describe how an overall pattern may be reflected in its component parts and how a 'récit absent' may be reconstituted from scattered clues and parallels. As in Van Eyck's portrait of the Arnolfini family, where a convex mirror provides a reduced and compressed image of the artist's subject, so the novelist will provide a compact, concentrated picture which the reader can magnify and fill out by responding imaginatively to the shrunken hints with which he is provided. The result is often inconclusive and puzzling, but far closer to the real world than the orderly patterns of tradition.

The 'New Realists' have never constituted a literary 'school', though the names of Robbe-Grillet, Nathalie Sarraute, Michel Butor and others were linked in the fifties and sixties as embodying a 'new wave'. For a time, Marguerite Duras was ranked with them, though it is now clear that she was — and remains — committed to a highly personal view of fiction which she has never defined or codified. Indeed, among major post-war literary figures in France, only Mme Duras and Samuel Beckett have not felt the need to set out a 'theory of the novel'. From her books we may detect practical sympathies with the movement — the demotion of the omniscient narrator, the search for 'inner realism', the taste for ellipsis and for that 'sous-dialogue' which says more than it seems to — but she has contributed a unique quality of detached and lucid passion which lends her fables a sense of urgency not always encountered elsewhere. Her fictions are neither complete nor self-contained. In each, it may be assumed that a question has been asked. Yet the nature and scope of the question remains elusive. The only certainty is that it is restated, its terms redefined, so that the reader is left staring at an uncertainty as he might stare at the Russian doll which is contained within itself: it is reduced, concentrated, different, and yet it is the same question. From book to book, Marguerite Duras speaks of love and liberty, of loving and liberation, of the oppression which is their antithesis, and to each she adds question marks which are so many aspirations to an absolute. From *Les Impudents* (1943) to her most recent films, she offers a slow unfolding of values, a succession of goals within goals, so real but so elusive that they are most clearly stated when they are most elusive. If the work of Mme Duras is 'difficult', it is because her goals and values are not easily reducible to simple statements. Her books and films are definitions of 'freedom' and 'love' infinitely more precise and subtle than the dictionary sense we are in the habit of giving them. The reader is called upon to give much of himself, for Mme Duras defines art as a collective conspiracy which places even greater burdens upon the act of reading than upon the act of writing. This means neither the abdication of the artist's responsibilities nor a concession to a fashion in obscurantism. It is simply that she seeks to avoid controlling our response to her novels in precisely the same way that our eyes are freed by her camera. Flaubert's wish to be transparent is nothing beside Mme Duras's wish to disappear from her fictions and leave them to her public.

Since her novels, plays, films and 'textes' are so many inter-slotting dolls which re-emerge, different but the same, it follows that the reader who selects a Duras title out of sequence places himself at a considerable disadvantage. To come to her at *Moderato cantabile,* the eighth of her books, can be a disorientating experience. Is Anne no more than a twentieth-century Madame Bovary unable to square her temperamental romanticism with the facts of her life? is the book a feminist tract in which Anne is vanquished by the power of a male-dominated society? is it a rejection of middle-class values as sharply observed as *Thérèse Desqueyroux?* or a case history which shows the disintegration of a personality driven to madness by inner oppressions and external pressures? or a more general protest against the social conformism which is expected of all of us? or a less overt political *caveat*? or a metaphysical statement of values which transcend any indi-

vidual life? *Moderato cantabile* can be a puzzling book because
it seems open to so many different interpretations. It will be
of help, therefore, if we first seek the cardinal points of the
Durassian universe which had already been fifteen years in
the making when *Moderato cantabile* was published in 1958.

2

Thematic and Structural Patterns

Mme Duras strenuously rejects labels and denies any suggestion that she was ever an 'écrivain de chapelle'. Her Vietnamese childhood and her mathematical and legal training constituted an unusually non-literary background for a writer: she claims to have read nothing seriously before the age of twenty. Yet she has remained grateful for her late start, since it meant that she began with few preconceptions and a general openness to new ideas. It is difficult to be categorical about the authors who 'influenced' her, though they would include Rousseau, Melville and Rimbaud, Gide and Kafka, Thomas Mann and Proust, Virginia Woolf and Ivy Compton-Burnett and the 'American' novels of Hemingway and Erskine Caldwell. But she has always responded quickly to changes in the intellectual climate — most recently she has taken up the feminist cause — which, filtered and adapted, she has absorbed and incorporated into a highly original and extremely personal body of writings which spans four decades.

Her childhood experience of life in a French colony has left her with an implacable hatred of injustice and oppression of all kinds which is at the root of her strong political views. During the War, she joined the French Communist Party from which she was expelled in 1950 for her failure to subordinate her left-wing principles to the party line. She has never broken with her communist ideals, though she has been an outspoken critic of the Marxist-Leninist philosophy of the Party which, in turn, has missed few opportunities for levelling the score.

During the War, she also became interested in existentialism and clear echoes of Camus and Sartre are detectable as late as *Le Marin de Gibraltar* (1952) whose narrator shares Meursault's responsiveness to physical sensations and embarks on a revolt against the numbing effects of routine and the commonsense world. Yet her 'existentialism' has been as unsystematic and idiosyncratic as her communism, though both must rank as keystones of her work which, while seemingly detached and objective, is an ardent expression of Mme Duras's obsessive personal values. With the exception of *Un Barrage contre le Pacifique* (1950), which traces her family's struggle to survive in Indo-China in the 1920s, none of her books is autobiographical in the documentary sense. Yet in everything she writes, she unveils her private self as she holds out the prospect of that 'impossible revolution' which is a promise of freedom and fulfilment.

Her first four novels were traditional in manner, though from the start her characters seek solutions to characteristically Durassian problems and speak the puzzling, elusive dialogue which has become her trademark as a writer of fiction. But her first books were also tentative in the sense that the 'Duras woman', who dominates the novels from *Les Petits Chevaux de Tarquinia* (1953), emerges from the shadow of an older, dominant brother-figure: in *La Vie tranquille* and *Un Barrage contre le Pacifique,* it is the brother who shows the heroine the way and in *Des Journées entières dans les arbres,* it is the son's revolt which defines the concept of emancipation. Similarly, in *Le Marin de Gibraltar,* though Anna may give the narrator a lead, her quest is modelled on the rebellion of the legionary she seeks. Though this enigmatic, strong male figure survives — Jacques in *Les Petits Chevaux,* Chauvin in *Moderato cantabile* and Roderigo in *Dix heures et demie du soir en été* (1960) — his importance declines as Mme Duras's heroines occupy the centre of her stage.

But if, by about 1953, the masculine element fades (to be replaced by children who play a similar, but less active role), so do the traditional features of her writing. Developed plots and characters begin to give way to the exploration of a static situation. The pattern changed with *Les Petits Chevaux* and has since become much refined. Her characters, with few exceptions middle-class women of thirty or so, oppressed by the prison of their personal and social circumstances, seek escape to a state of pure freedom which is usually seen in terms of love. By the end of the fifties, an act of violence — public as in *Hiroshima mon amour,* vicarious as in *Moderato* or personal as in *Les Viaducs de la Seine-et-Oise* — had become the necessary trigger for the escape mechanism. Subsequently, existential pressures drive Mme Duras's characters into a state of trance (or 'ravissement' (*17,* pp. 65-6) which, as we shall see, is equated with a kind of madness) where the way ahead is clearly marked. Specific acts of violence still occur in the later books — the eponymous hero of *Le Vice-Consul* fires on the lepers of Lahore — and other figures may use cruelty to give impetus to the heroine's revolt (as in *Détruire, dit-elle*), but the revolt itself has ceased to hinge primarily on sexual love and since the middle sixties has become an increasingly overt political gesture. The Duras woman's rebellion, her brief glimpse of a state of harmony between the self and the world, is presented as an act of revolt. After 1968, revolt turns into revolution and the harmony becomes part of a social vision which Mme Duras still pursues with undiminished zeal: the mysticism of her early books has become a more general goal which she herself concedes to be 'utopian' (*18,* pp. 114-15). Prejudices, tyrannies and hierarchies have replaced marriage and the unhappy, individual soul as the object of destruction. Mme Duras has collectivised her characters' search for emancipation: society must be destroyed, not by a bloody revolution, but by a spiritual renaissance. *Nathalie Granger* shows how women might take possession of their identity. In *Le Camion,* the proletarian driver is shown how left-wing ideology, committed to the struggle against the right, is no less oppressive than the old 'class' enemy it is pledged to destroy. Mme Duras clings to the glimpse of the 'impossible revolution' provided by the events of May 1968 which she saw, like many others, as a spontaneous act of revolt by students, workers and intellectuals. Since that date, her work has been profoundly influenced by a non-denominational political conviction — implicit, however, even in her early writings — that starts from the view that human nature is trapped in social chains which we can and must shake off.

This brief outline of the progressive politicisation of Mme Duras's values will remove Anne Desbaresdes from any simple comparison with Madame Bovary or Thérèse Desqueyroux. Anne does more than fight for her own liberty: her reactions are a cipher for a wider and more mystical act of rebellion. *Moderato cantabile* is a carefully constructed and subtly orchestrated book which will become accessible if first we isolate not only the essential mechanics of revolt but also the symbols which describe what lies beyond it.

1. 'L'ATTENTE'. The lives led by Mme Duras's characters, before their moment of revolt, are common, dull and respectable and take the form of a routine job or, more frequently, an average marriage. Their existence is neither unbearable, though it is oppressive, nor is it actively resisted. It is a state of *attente* — at most a mood of non-specific expectation, passively endured. Yet friction breeds *ennui* — more than boredom, a condition of profound frustration — which in turn breeds a desire to escape to a more harmonious state of being. The price, in terms of courage, is high and much has to be abandoned. The heroine of *Le Boa* learns to seek her way by observing the snake devour its prey and by responding to

> le monde de l'impérieux, le monde fatal, celui de l'espèce considérée comme fatalité, qui était le monde de l'avenir, lumineux et brûlant, chantant et criant, de beauté difficile, mais à la cruauté duquel, pour y accéder, on devait se faire, comme on devait se faire au spectacle des boas dévorateurs. Et je voyais se lever le monde de l'avenir de ma vie, du seul avenir possible de la vie, je le voyais ouvrir avec la musicalité, la pureté d'un déroulement de serpent, et il me semblait que, lorsque je le connaîtrais, ce serait de cette façon qu'il m'apparaîtrait, dans un développement d'une continuité majestueuse, où ma vie serait prise et reprise, et menée à son terme, dans des transports de terreur, de ravissement, sans repos, sans fatigue' (*6*, p. 115).

The movement towards this new lyrical freedom cannot be engineered by a conscious act of will, though it must be willed.

The phrase 'il suffit de vouloir' recurs with great regularity and is used to mean a high degree of instinctive volition, an obsessive groundswell of desire for escape, a passion for freedom. Without it, *l'attente* will be unfulfilled and *l'ennui* will continue as a standing function of existence. With it, the moment of release will come, in its own time, inevitably.

2. EXISTENCE AND IDENTITY. Francine, the heroine of Mme Duras's clearest 'existentialist' statement, *La Vie tranquille,* gradually perceives that her existence is precarious and that she misreads its terms. She comes to see that there is neither past nor future in any conventional sense, only an eternally renewed present. Actions mean little, for what was done yesterday was done by another 'I'. Yesterday's actions shape today — to this extent the past accidentally determines the present — yet they have consequences which are unforeseeable and beyond our control. What we do is therefore 'sans importance', since we can never be certain (as Sartre had demonstrated in *Le Mur*) that actions will produce the results we intend. We can do no more than resign ourselves to what has been and to its consequences until such time as we understand just how arbitrary our existence is. Our highly prized personal identity is an illusion, for we are no more in control of it than of the colour of our hair: it is in fact a 'social' identity, the product of random events and influences. Francine aspires to oneness with her lover, Tiène, but she lives each day in the existential void of ever-being and not-becoming.

Only the arbitrary phenomena of existence are real — hence Mme Duras's lack of interest in psychological motivation and her already noticeable refusal to provide specific explanations of her apparently random notations of speech and action — and Francine's awareness of her body is the one unarguable reality which allows her to experience the authentic 'joy' of existing. Her image in her mirror demonstrates that the space she occupies is a fact. Countless other selves, shaped by different pasts, might have inhabited her body, but she knows that only her consciousness fills the skin which contains it. It is not to a personal identity that she aspires: she longs to be as a drop of water in the sea, a constituent and totally assimilated part of Being itself. If Mme Duras's novels seem to put a premium upon re-shaping personal identity, her aim is really to destroy mere egocentrism and guide us towards a richer state of being which accords with the arbitrariness of existence itself.

3. 'ENNUI' AND REVOLT. Those who wait, wait passively, though their passivity is not inert. They wait uneasily, constrained by external pressures which seek to mould them into the limiting patterns of social and moral conformity. The pressures come variously from a routine job, family life or the distance which separates a love affair from Love itself. All such forms of coercion are, in Mme Duras's view, political, and in her later books she displays a violent antipathy to all forms of authority and hierarchy which deny both freedom and individuality. By 'politics' is meant opposition to those social, moral, economic and other pressures which are used by the collectivity to foster particular norms of behaviour. The specific orthodoxy of the State is immaterial, for Mme Duras has come to believe that any ideology turns into a system which degenerates into tyranny. In this sense, the tyranny of the right is indistinguishable from that of the left.

The experience of *ennui* is thus crucial, for it helps to locate and identify those forces of oppression which must be resisted by an act of revolt. To resist is inevitably a political act. In *Un Barrage contre le Pacifique,* Joseph frees himself when he fires on the government agent, but his revolt — a rejection of the system which enslaves his existence — is a protest against all systems.

4. TIME. The time of waiting is long and undifferentiated, a grey waste of unthinking response. But as the movement towards revolt begins, time expands with consciousness and fills more than the temporal units by which we normally measure it. The developed plots of Mme Duras's first books set out the immediate context of revolt. But by *Les Petits Chevaux de Tarquinia* the circumstantial context has become irrelevant

and henceforth the crisis of revolt occupies a few days, an afternoon, a couple of hours and fills an unreal moment with speculation, memory and action until past and future disappear leaving only the endless present which is itself a glimpse of the absolute. The end of waiting *(la durée)* and the gesture of revolt *(le moment)* constitute the basic structural articulation of Mme Duras's fiction. This explains the absence of psychology and motivation: Mme Duras is not concerned with elucidating the present by means of the past but with showing her characters at the moment of their escape.

5. NATURE. This lack of interest in the circumstantial and the anecdotal means that the description of setting, dress and gesture (traditionally used as explanatory devices) is downgraded until it becomes as functional as the briefest stage dircction. Whereas Balzac, in *Le Père Goriot,* describes the Pension Vauquer in such detail that it is differentiated from all other boarding houses, Mme Duras refuses to anchor her characters in a specific physical context and merely indicates that the action of her stories takes place on a park bench in an anonymous town, on a beach which is any beach or in a Calcutta which is historically and geographically 'false'. Only in one respect is background given any depth. There are frequent and insistent references to the weather which stress heat, follow the progress of the sun or mark the onset of an evening breeze. Such indications, far from being random, are intended as a necessary counterpoint, a means of suggesting both the stifling predicament of her characters and also the imminence of relief. The sea too is omnipresent, a living force which beckons with a massive assertion of an alternative and freer state of being: the mother, in *Un Barrage contre le Pacifique,* attempts to resist the sea and is defeated. Trees and forests, as cruel and mysterious as the sea, are similar reminders of the pure Being which contrasts with the oppressions of the commonsense world. Winds rustle in trees, suns set over seas, forests have 'une profondeur marine' and sea-beds may look like forests — a constant conjunction of symbols which highlights the complicity of the physical world. Sara, of *Les*

Petits Chevaux de Tarquinia, swims underwater and sees
'l'envers du monde', a negative image of conventional reality,
a 'monde renversé' where she feels at peace and at one with
the very springs of existence. Mme Duras may neglect the
man-made world, but she evokes the physical world as a
powerful symbol of her values.

6. MATERNITY AND THE CHILD. Mme Duras has said that
'toute maternité est dramatique' (*17,* pp. 105-6). It is not
surprising therefore if mothers and their children figure
prominently in her work. The child exists in a state of innocence, as yet unshaped by the conforming pressures of the
adult world. 'L'enfant est un fou, complètement, qui s'assagit'
(*17,* p. 125), a free creature who reaches an accommodation
with life and, in the process, loses his innocence. There is no
morality in the child; he accepts what is, unthinkingly. In this
sense, he is the human representative of the values expressed
by seas and forests. The experience of motherhood is crucial
for it enables a mother to regain contact with her own lost
childhood freedom from oppression and the norms of 'reasonable' thinking. Nathalie Granger's resistance to school and her
piano lessons thus constitute a revolt against the forces of
corruption, while, in *Des Journées entières dans les arbres,*
Jacques's mother experiences joy when she understands that
his boyhood wildness and brutality have not been compromised
by the attractions of a career and social success. In a very
literal sense, Mme Duras wishes us to recapture the ability to
see with the eyes of a child.

7. TRIGGERS. Thus far we have seen how Mme Duras
defines oppression and the surge of resistance which springs
from inner longings, conscious protest and the beckonings of
nature. But before the mechanism of revolt may be unleashed,
a trigger is required. It may be the cinema which Mme Duras
has described as 'une forme de bonheur', for however escapist
the film, the act of watching a bright screen in a dark room affords a glimpse of another, more harmonious world. Music,
often in the form of a popular tune, raises hopes of a more

lyrical existence and gives a specific resonance to the absolute. Alcohol too releases inhibitions, weakens accepted morality and provides the courage needed for resistance and revolt. In the same way, place — or rather displacement — may turn *ennui* into *le refus*. Mme Duras regularly situates her characters in ill-defined or neutral settings (a park, a boat, or the beach/ seaside town which is half-way between land and sea) where habit and routine are weakest: a holiday, with its unaccustomed heat, new sensations and general rootlessness, disrupts the individual's normal habits and forces him to see things with new eyes. Several triggers may be required — sexual desire, a sudden understanding of the power of the sea or the forest or the innocence of the child — but once they have been activated the process of change is inevitable.

8.   FEAR. Though 'il suffit de vouloir', release is not easily achieved. Though escape is ardently desired, it involves the abandonment of past values and habits, and a 'voyage' across a sea which is uncharted, the negative image of what has hitherto been known and accepted. Thus, even as the goal is perceived, fear of the unknown or of the goal itself is a common reaction. It is a dread of the enormity of the task of leaving the familiar world, a fear of the exhilarating state of freedom which awaits. Liberation through revolt is the highest imperative, but to attain it the individual must first conquer the fear of freedom.

9.   IMPRUDENCE. Passively fearing, as they once passively accommodated their *ennui,* Mme Duras's characters, under the influence of heat or music or holidays or alcohol, reach a point at which only an imprudent action will enable them to abandon their oppressive lives. The act may be relatively anodyne — giving up one's job, for instance — but it may involve immorality (adultery, for example) and even crime. They commit unwise, wild and sometimes brutal actions which deny the prudence and conformity of accepted social and moral standards: they behave like the 'serpent dévorateur' of *Le Boa.* Joseph fires on the government inspector as later the Vice

Consul shoots at the lepers of Lahore; Claire Lannes dis-
members her cousin and Anne Desbaresdes re-enacts a murder
in which she is the victim. But whatever the degree of imprudence, an act of destruction is always involved: the old
way of looking at the world must be expunged and replaced
by a new manner of seeing. If the means are violent, it is
because so profound a revolution cannot otherwise be achieved.

10. LOOKING AND SEEING. Mme Duras's characters inhabit
a world which they no longer perceive with clarity, for they
overlay it with routine, rationalisation and habit; they re-order
it to make it consistent with their weaknesses and the need
for conformity. It frequently happens therefore that they look
— as we do — without seeing; the significance of what they
observe is not explained and the reader, in his puzzlement, is
encouraged to look for himself. But when the moment of
release comes, it is because what has been merely looked at
has been *seen* in the clearest light. A situation becomes transparent, or rather its reverse image appears and with it the
superior, inverted values of a 'monde renversé'. When the act
of revolt arrives, looking ceases and a cleaner, purer vision
takes its place. 'Voir, ça s'apprend,' says Mme Duras and her
books are an instruction in the clear perception of existence.

11. 'L'IMPOSSIBLE'. The spiritual and emotional odyssey
chronicled by Mme Duras is complex: the journey is difficult
and the goal elusive. Many of her early stories centre upon
love as the later fictions focus upon more overtly political
rebellions, but the 'impossibility' of realisation is always the
same. For her heroines, the absolute is a generous, complete
vision of Love itself which is, by definition, unattainable: to
love one man is to limit Love, just as even a happy marriage
is a denial of the full potential of Happiness. Childhood innocence does not survive the growing child any more than a
utopian vision of freedom can be realised by recourse to
politics. It is in this sense that Mme Duras speaks of 'l'amour
impossible' and 'la révolution impossible', though she does not
suggest for one moment that they are beyond our reach. It is

rather that to achieve the impossible, we must abandon established modes of thought and the structural patterns of organised society — education which destroys innocence, marriage which sets limits on love, and politics which turns even the most generous visions into crabbed tyrannies. It is a revolt so profound but so necessary that for most people it is unthinkable. *Détruire, dit-elle,* written in the aftermath of May 1968 when such a revolution seemed not only possible but to have begun, states the case for the destruction of the bankrupt past, a vital act of emancipation. Yet the profound transformation of values that seemed imminent failed to materialise and the 'impossibility' of revolution seems as great now as the 'impossibility' of Love did to her first heroines.

12. 'UN CRI PUR'. There comes a moment, therefore, when the realisation that the vision is 'impossible' to translate into real and lasting form, becomes intolerable. At such a moment, the only reaction possible is limited to a pure, animal scream. Francine, in *La Vie tranquille,* nears this stage and explains that 'il m'aurait servi de vivre pour nourrir de toute ma force ce cri-là. Je serais cri. Mon âge volerait en poussières et le monde, et le Bon et l'Infâme, et toute définition. Ah! je pourrais enfin mourir en un cri. Sans pensée, sans sagesse, je ne serais que ce cri de joie d'avoir à mourir en un cri' (p. 173). From the travel-obsessed narrator of *Le Marin de Gibraltar* ('Si j'avais crié, je n'aurais certainement rien pu sortir d'autre que des sons inarticulés, "yacht," par exemple' (p. 98)) to the Vice Consul howling in the gardens of the French Embassy at Calcutta, the pain of liberation rings loud and true. For the scream does not signify despair or disillusionment; once glimpsed, the absolute is irresistible. Rather it marks an intense awareness of the plenitude of existence and of the distance which separates this new state of consciousness from those who have turned their backs on the old oppressions and have begun to make themselves free.

13. MADNESS. The act of revolt is conceived in a state of imprudence, the incautious rejection of common values. It is a

break with identity, the self and the conscious will. But above all, it is a flight from reason. Rational thought is the greatest single obstacle to liberation: 'l'intelligence a ses habitudes de pensée qui l'empêchent d'apercevoir ses propres conditions' *(3, p. 55)*. The way lies rather along the path of unreason which ceases to be the opposite of reason and emerges as a new lucidity. 'Il n'y a qu'à épier la folie sans esprit de raison et alors elle s'explique d'elle-même, se fait comprendre' *(2, p. 210)*. To remain reasonable is to consent to the old slaveries; madness is the key to freedom. From the earliest books, Mme Duras's characters show a weak grasp of conventional modes of thought and a readiness to react against them rashly and sometimes violently. They follow an alternative logic which is rooted in the view that man, far from being the master of his destiny, is the fool of his intelligence. Rational principles, organised systems and self-imposed structures are so many weapons which turn against man himself, denying his need for liberty and for peaceful co-existence with his being. Reason is thus rejected in favour of madness, the new and ultra-clear form of seeing, and an instinctive immorality emerges as the new morality. In the works published during the fifties, madness is rarely more than a cipher for the revolt against reason. Subsequently, it has figured much more prominently in heroines like Claire Lannes and Lol V. Stein who escape the intolerable burden of their lives into a trance-like connivance with their true Being. To be 'mad' as Mme Duras understands the word, is to rise above the 'esprit de raison' and to be as water in the sea.

14. SUBSTITUTIONS: 'LE VOYEUR'. Since love and revolution are 'impossible', the Duras woman does not attempt to exploit her new freedom in any personal way nor does she make any proprietary claims upon it. She is content to be part of her new vision, to be assimilated into existence itself. Fundamentally a contemplative, she lives 'à travers les autres', remaining within sight of their freedom in a state of permanent 'joy', the moment made durable. The early heroines identify with a dominant brother whose urge to freedom, though more aggressive and assertive, represents a surrogate form of exis-

tence. The narrator of *Le Marin de Gibraltar* acts as a replacement for Anna's lost sailor and provides love against a background of Love. Monsieur Andesmas, who refuses to see that his daughter has grown away from him, looks at the little girl who visits him and confuses her with Valerie. On a quite different level, the atomic catastrophe of *Hiroshima mon amour* is interchangeable with the private catastrophe of Nevers. For these parallelisms and substitutions, Mme Duras now uses the word 'voyeurism', by which she means a state of lucid yet personal seeing. The function of Stein in *Détruire, dit-elle,* is that of *voyeur:* by observing, he maintains the intensity of the desire which would otherwise be lost in the couple Elisabeth/ Thor. In the same way, Lol V. Stein stares at the window of the hotel room where her former lover has a rendez-vous with her friend: Lol has been rejected but retains a high awareness of Love in which she now participates, 'voyeuristically', through an act of love committed by others. It is in the voyeur's trance that the Duras woman experiences fully and permanently what is otherwise fleeting and elusive. The Durassian voyeur *sees* and no longer needs to look.

15.   DEATH. Freedom, Mme Duras has said, is as much feared by society as madness and death. The urge to freedom is in this sense a form of suicide, 'un suicide de tous les autres possibles de soi' (*17,* p. 55). It is a refusal to be anything other than oneself, and choosing to be oneself, as Francine's mirror image confirms, means murdering one's conscious identity which is the sum of our past and of our acceptance of the common oppressions. To be oneself is to kill the egocentric self, to become 'dead'. It is only after this 'death' that there can arise a new awareness of life itself, of its richness and simplicity. The Duras woman dies therefore only to be prepared for true existence. It is in this sense that the Vice Consul 'est mort, il n'est pas mort, c'est-à-dire, il est la vie même, puisqu'il ne peut rien supporter, la vie étant exprimable par le refus, chez moi. Plus tu refuses, plus tu es opposé, plus tu vis' (*17,* p. 173). To die is to be reborn and death is a great victory.

* * *

For nearly forty years, Marguerite Duras has been working towards a goal which is no less than the repossession of the self. Her work puts forward a philosophy of resistance and revolt which has points of contact with other existentialist doctrines, but is in the last analysis a personal and generous libertarian theorem. Although the cycle of waking, rebirth and contemplation might appear to amount to a spiritual renaissance, the equivalent of a mystical, religious experience, Mme Duras firmly dissociates herself from religion. Instead, she characterises her work as political in a very wide sense. In her view, party politics and ideologies are irrelevant and she calls for deep revolutionary changes of a somewhat diffuse nature and an end to prejudice, fear and the growing tyrannies imposed by the collectivity. She looks forward to 'a new state of the human being, man and woman. It is yet unforeseeable, but it will probably consist — for 80% at least — in the destruction of conceit, of selfishness, of "virility" so praised by mothers of warriors, by heads of state and chiefs in general whether they be Fascist or Socialist' (*32,* p. 8). If a 'revolution of love' seems a less than specific political goal, Mme Duras has indicated that certain of her ideals were enshrined in the Hippie movement of the late sixties which she views as a spontaneous rejection of materialism and establishment values. In a sense, it is a romantic quest aimed at rescuing the individual from society, and indeed her assumption that nature is superior to man-made systems, that emotion is more vital than reason and that political structures degenerate into tyranny recalls the anti-intellectual stance of Rousseau.

Mme Duras is no rational thinker (she has never attempted a theorical exposition of her ideas) nor has she any abstract view on the nature of fiction: what she has to say must stand or fall in the form she has given them. However, she has many times discussed her books and from her comments it is clear that the experimental nature of her narratives is a central part of her philosophical purpose. Just as she seeks to destroy society, so she sets out to destroy the traditional novel with its 'bavardage romanesque' and misleading mission to represent reality. If she now rejects all she wrote before *Moderato cantabile,* it is because her early books were too clear, too linear, and left nothing unsaid. Her 'théorie des blancs' explains why the texts published since *Moderato* have been more allusive and more difficult. By omitting narrative stages, by suppressing actions and reactions, Mme Duras believes that she can bring what is crucial into much clearer focus. For instance, while there is much intense, dramatic emotion in her books, there is little feeling, for feelings of regret or longing would obscure the pain of revolt and the joy of release. More is involved than the new novel's rejection of traditional psychology and plot, for Mme Duras passes over events which crystallise revolt — her murders occur off-stage and belong to another story — and she even omits characters (like Valerie in *L'Après-midi de Monsieur Andesmas*) who are the focal point of her protagonist's rebirth. The 'personnage absent' and the 'récit absent' are central techniques through which our attention is directed towards the essence of her dramas and away from their distracting, anecdotal circumstances. This is why she has claimed that *Détruire, dit-elle* is no more than a 'preamble' to a more significant story which begins after her novel ends: what we see in a Duras novel must be supplemented with a number of 'récits absents' implied in the text. Just as her descriptions are reduced to a handful of 'signs' which the reader is required to turn into mental pictures ('J'appelle cette méthode qui est la mienne descriptions par touches de couleur' (*31,* p. 655)), so we are intended to see her novels as photographic negatives from which we must invent the real story which lies beyond the story we read.

The 'théorie des blancs' clearly accounts for the elliptical bias of Mme Duras's writing, though decipherment of the 'blancs' is made easier by recurring narrative patterns and the systematic cross-referencing of significant incident. Settings vary — a café, a park, a clinic — but are always chosen to suggest uprooted, receptive states of mind. Climatic variations are carefully noted but the effect is to define the object of the rebellion which takes place. Piano lessons symbolise attempts

to erode the innocence of the child. Eating serves as a gas-
tronomical instance of a more general violence while bouts of
vomiting provide a dramatic image of rejection. Substitutions
and parallels create multiple resonances within a framework of
repeated actions and reactions which assume an incantatory
value. Stories and parts of stories end as they began and the
same ground may be covered several times in a slowly turning
spiral. Clarity, which Mme Duras denies us, emerges from
confusions, strange identifications and her insistence that crucial
moments are most dramatically rendered in a mood of under-
statement. For her narratives are as compact and tense as a
Racinian tragedy with which, in their respect for the unities
of time, place and action, they have much in common. Reduced
to bare essentials — situation replaces plot, the 'touches de
couleur' take over from description, the 'moment of becoming'
makes the old psychological approach to character redundant
— her novels and films are the expression of a temperamental
litotes.

But the most noticeable feature of all, perhaps, is the
capital role Mme Duras attributes to dialogue. While it is
undeniable that the shift away from description reflects her
long-standing fascination with the cinema, the attractions of
the *ciné-roman* as a form do not alone explain why she has
chosen to place the burden of her narrative more and more
upon dialogue. Her characters rarely speak to each other but
indulge a private *monologue à deux,* a series of seemingly
random exchanges which chart the growth of revolt. A remark
may strike an obsessive chord and the reply is not an answer
but the exploration of a private obsession: dialogue is given
pride of place because it is the most revealing instrument of
self-knowledge. A Duras dialogue is a series of non-sequiturs
imbued with an inner logic which becomes clear only when
we understand that her characters do not speak to each other,
but to themselves and to us. The reader is the indispensable
eavesdropper who gives point to what is seemingly pointless,
just as only the reader can shape the scattered symbols and
substitutions into a clear perception of the revolt which unfolds

before him. What this means is that Mme Duras opens the novel to the reader just as she gives her films to her public. She has no desire to tell us anything. Her aim is to make us see as clearly as her liberated heroes see when at last they contemplate the fullness of their new freedom.

3

Moderato cantabile, an ´expérience intérieure´

DIABELLI directed that his sonatina, *opus* 168, no. 1, be played at a moderate pace and 'in a singing manner'. Mme Duras directs us to read her novel in precisely the same mood of sympathetic but measured calm which seems oddly at variance with the violence and drama which lie just beneath the surface of the story she tells. Indeed, as a direction, *moderato cantabile* mobilises qualitatively different though not irreconcilable responses: strict tempo and personal expression, control and freedom, detachment and involvement, reason and emotion. It starts, if not a paradox, then at least a tension which is at the heart of the book. The structure, drama and meaning of the novel are articulated according to this basic dialectical pattern and the process begins in chapter one.

I.   The opening pages create an atmosphere which is made of oppressions, some more visible than others. The child is scolded, though he remains the self-contained and untroubled centre of the tensions surrounding the ritual of the piano lesson. Mlle Giraud shouts and is driven to anger by his passive resistance and by the 'aridity' of her role as a teacher who, with each new pupil, must transform innocence and spontaneity into conforming patterns laid down by society. Loveless and sour, she is oppressed by her impotence and by the destructiveness of this lesson in which she figures as the representative of establishment values, one form of the *moderato* of the title. Anne Desbaresdes, meanwhile, basks uncomfortably in a state of uncertainty, at times weakly conniving with Mlle Giraud, at others rejoicing in the boy's obstinacy. For behind her acceptance of the view that music lessons are part of the preparation for adulthood, lies a profounder complicity with the child's unshaped innocence and she responds with wonderment to this being who exists in complete harmony with himself and to whom she is bound by the ties of motherhood. Anne is a watcher and in her *attente* she half-perceives the perfection of being which waits beyond the limits of her daily life.

For if Mlle Giraud's room is enclosed and sterile, the boy does not feel its oppressions. He exists in a world of light and air. Only he is aware that the evening has 'exploded', only he feels the passing boat stir in his blood (though Anne senses his reaction). His gestures are unconscious and 'innocent' and he responds instinctively to the call of the sea and the sunset which, in turn, beckon to him and fill his hair with light. For outside the room and beyond the 'moderate' town lies the 'singing' natural world which, though kept at bay and observed only through Mlle Giraud's window, is never more insistent than in the child's silence which is the expression of his refusal to co-operate. The sea is loudest and the sunset most striking when he shapes for his act of rebellion: 'Je ne veux pas apprendre le piano' (p. 13; 10). It is at this same instant that the scream blots out all sound as suddenly the complicity of nature, the child's revolt and an act of murder combine to thrust the drama into a higher musical key. Fear drives the child to withdraw his challenge and fear makes Anne seek the protection of conformity; simultaneously the power goes out of the sunset, leaving a void in which the violence reverberates. As 'le rose du ciel' grows fainter, the sound of the sea is replaced by the murmur of the crowd which is in turn overlaid by the sonatina, the symbol of the child's defeat, which is itself overcome by the 'imperious' clamour of voices which beckon us towards the drama that has happened on the other side of the window, between Mlle Giraud's room and the sea. The child was afraid and capitulated. Anne too felt fear but now surrenders — in the 'sourire d'un enfantement sans fin' which is an echo of the scream she has heard — to something purer even than the child's innocence which has now lost something of its power: she is repelled by the ease with which he now obeys his teacher. His sonatina, played at a moderate tempo and 'in a singing manner', no longer rises above the noise of the crowd and Anne submits to the movement which, since the beginning of the chapter, has tempted us to leave Mlle Giraud's room for the world outside which calls through her window.

The 'événement inconnu' to which she is drawn is the aftermath of a *crime passionnel*. The crime itself belongs to the past but the passion remains: the 'actualité', of the murder has been assimilated by the crowd which, however, does not understand its significance. The background is full of sound and movement — the police come and go, the *patronne* is shrill, the photographer unfeelingly points his camera and unidentified voices say 'pauvre femme' and 'c'est dégoûtant' — but the man who occupies the foreground is calm and self-contained, stirring occasionally as if to threaten more violence which, however, does not materialise. The police and the spectators are concerned with what has happened, with the 'récit absent' which, like the crowd's reactions, fills only the periphery of what we see. At the still centre of the scene is the man etched vividly in the camera flash, smiling, clinging to the woman he has murdered, completely absorbed in his desire. It is as though he has achieved perfect love through death and is dazzled by an awareness of being at one with an absolute in a way which is not possible in life. Who he is and what he has done is unimportant beside what he now sees. He has withdrawn into a 'monde renversé' where 'dignity' and his own fate are irrelevant, into a state of 'délire' which is the liberating condition of 'madness': death itself is transcended for he is unaware of the distinction between a living and a dead body.

The policemen are bored and the crowd shows vague sympathy and, more markedly, a ghoulish interest in the murder, a crude curiosity far removed from the 'voyeurism' required for an understanding of the man's conduct and remoteness. Anne may sense that the murder is not the end of love but its ultimate incarnation, yet we see nothing of her reactions save her question: 'Pourquoi?', to which she receives no answer. To the child, who is as lost in his own world as the murderer is in his, she is brisk and there is even a hint of impatience in her voice as she tells him that *moderato* means 'modéré' and *cantabile* means 'chantant'. Perhaps she senses that the 'mon amour' which she has called the child hardly bears comparision with the 'mon amour, mon amour' of the murderer, for the child has ceased to be her only intimation of perfect love.

II. The second chapter confirms that Anne has been profoundly affected by the murder. Casually, as if on the spur of the moment, she returns to the café, a no-man's land midway between the town and her large house at the end of the Boulevard de la Mer — a variant of the neutral parks and the sea-shore where she often takes her son and where her social identity is weakened by the absence of the familiar props of her daily existence. She is aware that by responding to a mysterious call, she is living dangerously: as she crosses the threshold, she commits her first imprudent act.

Though outwardly composed, she is ill at ease, not merely because a woman in her position does not drink cheap wine in a workman's café, but because she cannot help herself. Her hands tremble as she drinks in order to find the courage to face her fear. She talks to cover her discomfiture, answers unasked questions, justifies herself and lies to hide her vulnerability and her passionate need to know. So strong is her desire to feel what she has seen in the man's eyes that not only does her hold on reality become precarious (she has difficulty in responding to banal remarks) but she also ceases to be aware of the spontaneous 'abandon heureux' of her son: she gives him perfunctory answers and her gestures towards him are 'distraits' and mechanical. The well-regulated life of the bar surrounds her yet its reality recedes as she drinks. The curiosity of the *patronne* and the surprise of the customers fade as she surrenders to the surging vision within her. If she maintains partial contact with her surroundings, it is due less to her ingrained courtesy, a kind of dignity, than to her need to know 'why'.

More real, therefore, than the busy café or even her child is the polite man who has approached her and speaks authoritatively on the only subject which interests her. It is clear to

us that he knows no more than Anne could have guessed or
read in a newspaper. His authority does not derive from his
knowledge but from his intuitive understanding of her obsessive
interest in the murder. He says what we know already
('C'était un crime', 'elle est morte'), what we guessed ('il est
maintenant devenu fou') and what may be disputed (we heard
the scream but did not hear a shot, nor can we be sure that
'lui le savait', pp. 25-7; 18-20). The *patronne* adds that the
woman was married, had three children and drank, prosaic
facts which Anne rejects as irrelevant. For she requires a more
mystical and less banal explanation. She needs to know that
the murderer shot his mistress 'through the heart', that 'ils
s'aimaient', that the final act of love grew out of despair. She
seeks a pure apprehension of pure love.

Thus far, the man has prompted Anne's tentative probings,
placing words like so many signals to which she eagerly
responds. But now that the theme of Anne's quest has been
stated, there is a change of key and the theme is restated in
counterpoint to her own life. 'Il y a longtemps que vous pro-
menez votre enfant' (p. 29; 22), he says, a simple statement
which forces Anne to connect what has begun to emerge with
her own existence. Her answers are slow and oblique not only
because of her growing intoxication but because of the effort
she must make to relate her own consciousness to the reality
of a superior state of being. As she wanders, stupefied by
alcohol, he repeats his statement, reminds her of her social
identity ('Vous êtes Mme Desbaresdes', p. 31; 23) and talks
of her 'belle maison' and the garden which is as closed as her
life. Anne evades the issue, substituting the 'amour impossible'
she feels for her child for the vision the man has encouraged
her to see. But out of his insistence, out of the juxtaposition
of the vision and Anne's life, emerges a new tension. She
begins to look at the man whose eyes are fixed upon her and,
suddenly emerging from her self-absorption, becomes aware of
his presence and begins to draw him into the inner world
which blinds her with brilliant images of the murder which
took place — as we are reminded by a burst of sunlight which
now strikes the man's face — precisely twenty four hours

before. At this moment, he adds that the murderer aimed at the heart as the woman had asked. Anne gives a 'plainte presque licencieuse' (p. 33; 24) which is much stronger than the 'sourire d'enfantement' of the previous day. The murder is tentatively re-enacted and so strong is the identification that Anne ceases to be a watcher and becomes part of what she has seen.

But the release is momentary and lasts only until the man turns his eyes away. Anne slowly regains her composure and leaves the bar to the man who is as uninterested in hearing facts about her as she was in listening to the *patronne*'s information about the dead woman. She is overcome by a sense of the magical purity of the boy whose mouth is filled with sunlight: her wonderment has been renewed by her contact with the springs of life itself. Perhaps she invented him, as she is on the way to inventing the murder which has taken place.

III.   The second interview emphasises the ritual nature of the contact between Anne and the man. The walk, the weak protest of the child, the bar with its routine and noise, are the *obbligato* over which the contrapuntal themes of oppression and release are restated. There are formalities which must be observed: the wine drunk at the counter, the polite exchanges with the *patronne* and the patient waiting for the man to make the first move which acknowledges his status as the dominant partner. If chapter two tentatively re-enacted the murder, chapter three re-enacts the first meeting. The preliminaries are mechanical but the mood is charged with tension: both are pale beneath their calm exteriors. Their apparently trivial conversation is punctuated by apparently banal sounds and movements which, however, have a clear symbolic value. Barges are unloaded and tugs arrive just as Anne seeks to unburden herself by responding to the man's lead. Man-made smoke turns the sky into an angry, threatening backdrop, but as the interview ends the sky is clear and blue once more. As Anne moves nearer her liberation, the workmen arrive, released from their labours, and the child comes and goes happily, an image of the harmony which Anne wishes to attain. The external world is carefully exploited as a source of artful contrasts and revealing complicities.

The man remarks that three days have passed, a statement of fact which is a challenge on two levels: it reactivates their earlier mood and is a reproach directed against Anne's lack of courage which her failure to return clearly suggests. With 'une hypocrite timidité', she does not respond but seeks to divert attention from herself by taking refuge in her social identity: she makes polite enquiries about the man and intimates that her absence is to be explained solely in terms of etiquette. The man refuses to be drawn. He forces Anne to re-invent the murder for herself and out of her memory of different pasts she links the scream she has heard with the screams she herself uttered in childbed: the pain, she realises, came not from death but from life itself. It is a sudden intuition which frees her from fear and it is at this moment, when the first step in identification has been taken, that the man attacks: 'Parlez-moi' (p. 41; 30).

Again Anne responds, not without a great effort of concentration, and again she diverts attention from her true object by speaking of her social persona as symbolised by her house. But the man fastens unerringly on the magnolia tree which flowers inside the gate just as Anne's sensuality, which it symbolises, is imprisoned in her house 'où on vous a épousée' (p. 42; 31), an unusual turn of phrase which transforms Anne into the victim of her husband and her milieu. She is troubled by the remembered odour of the magnolia but again attempts to divert the conversation by returning to the murder. The man brushes her questions aside, giving a specifically sexual connotation to her sleepless nights and forcing her to revert to the house where she is both with her husband and apart from him. Nor does he encourage her to pursue the murdered woman's motivation, for such things are not be to explained in rational terms though they may be 'discovered' through intuitions. Relentlessly pursuing Anne's sexuality which she refuses to face, he reminds her that the murderer had felt as the woman had felt and he carefully sows the idea that their mood was not totally distinct from the relationship which is developing between them. Anne again resists, clinging to the 'methodical' approach of reason and taking refuge in her child, through whom she feels more safely in tune with the mysteries she is obsessively driven to pierce. The man reinforces the nascent identification of Anne with the woman, but it is the memory of a violent winter storm that had shattered her window panes (the frontier between Anne and the magnolia, the house and the sea, *ennui* and the absolute) which now leads to the intuitive 'discovery' that the absolute is real for the simple reason that it has materialised in this town, in this café. It is an illumination as crucial as the assimilation of the scream into her own experience of childbirth and in its light their 'ombres conjuguées' are projected against the wall. The man senses an advantage: 'Parlez-moi', he says (p. 45; 33).

But again, with great effort, she retreats into her social identity which the man punctures with much more open reminders of her sexuality: the heat, the magnolia, the 'robe décolletée'. Anne withdraws and dissembles but her ability to separate the murder from her sexuality now weakens to the point where past and present become confused. And the child, whose birth some ten years before was a first contact with the absolute, becomes the promise of future fulfilment: as he grows, so will her escape become complete. At this juncture of times, the man's hand lies next to hers and she grows aware of his existence. Remorselessly destroying her defences, he forces her to admit her sexual interest in the men whom she observes — through the window that overlooks the sea — and who disturb her nights. This confession, a further crucial step along the road to emancipation, coincides with a sudden awareness that the man is young and that the sun shines into his 'child's eyes' (p. 48; 35). It is a moment of intuitive insight in which Anne's sexuality, the approval of nature and the purity of childhood combine to confirm Anne in her quest for self-fulfilment. And if she feels a chill of fear, she is totally reassured as she surrenders to the purity of the child who is becoming a man: again she almost 'screams' and she whispers 'mon amour'. She acknowledges the boy's symbolic role as a present confirmation of her future liberation by promising to buy him a motor-boat the colour of blood, which is a cipher both of his freedom and of her inevitable emancipation.

IV. The third interview takes place the following day under the blue sky of an unaccustomed fine spell which, like Anne's situation, may continue for some time or suddenly end. Nature reflects the alternatives open to her and again the 'pénombre' in which their meeting begins will be despatched by the setting sun. Anne goes through the now 'ceremonial' preliminaries — already she is acquiring new habits — and other familiar rituals are repeated: the factory siren which marks the urgency of her search; the disapproval of the *patronne* and her customers; the interruptions of the child who has already found happiness with a companion; the red knitting which symbolises not only the routines of 'moderate' living but also murder and passion. Anne even repeats the same opening words, though now her remarks ('Je voudrais un autre verre de vin', 'Je n'ai pas l'habitude') take on a new significance. Her drinking has begun to be a compulsion, a new habit which will replace the bourgeois habits which have made her a prisoner of her 'moderate' life.

Her mood is easy, a little gay even. She is unconcerned by what people will say and is surprised that her fear has subsided. But the man begins exactly where they had broken off and further disturbs her mood by materialising suddenly as one of the nocturnal passers-by who now cease to be anonymous and unreal. Unable to accept the ease with which her remembered past has caught up with the living present, she drinks and then, guiltily, returns to the murder. The man simply confirms what is implicit in her question: release can come only when the time for talking is over. To know when that moment will come is now her uppermost obsession and the man draws her on by forcing her to see the couple still talking, as though the murder has yet to occur, working helplessly towards an inevitable conclusion which may still be months away. But with the 'implacable précision' of chance — fate and destiny have no part in this human drama — the sun lights the man's face as he returns to the destruction of Anne's identity (p. 55; 41).

Her garden and the way of life it represents have been a prison to which she never had the will to object. The beech obstructs her view of the sea but she never thought to have it removed. To combat her passivity, the man observes that she must be happy with things as they are and repeats what the *patronne* has said, that the dead woman drank, hung around bars and got herself talked about. It is a description which fits Anne's new 'vulgar' habits, but again she rejects the identification of which she is not yet conscious. But his remarks have weakened her assurance and again he strikes: 'Parlez-moi'.

Once more, with considerable difficulty, she speaks of the drunks who pass her house — not to stir memories but to justify her new habit. Alcohol gives them the courage to go beyond the limits of the town as she hopes to have the strength to go beyond the known. But it is to her sexuality that he returns: 'vous êtes couchée', he says, gathering her past into a general statement; 'vous étiez couchée', he adds with a switch of tenses which particularises her desire. Her self-protective detachment is threatened as her passionate nature stirs; her acceptance of habit has overlain her yearnings and life has passed her by. It is a thought which starts fear in her, fear of the unknown. It is now, when Anne is vulnerable, ready to abandon old habits but resistant to new ones, that the man personalises her sexuality and gives himself a name (p. 57; 42). But it is not his presence that affects her most but this reminder that Chauvin is a man who, in giving up his job at the Usines Desbaresdes, has asserted his freedom; the child is free by nature, the lovers freed themselves here, in this café, and now Chauvin not only sheds his anonymity but sits before her as one who has denied the oppression from which she herself seeks to escape. Chauvin follows up his advantage: 'Parlez-moi encore' (p. 58; 43).

Her ability to keep a safe distance between her longings and her life begins to weaken. She speaks of her past as though reciting a lesson concerning matters which do not concern her. Habit has protected her against her imprisoned life and it is to rational habits of mind that she now looks as a defence against Chauvin. She resists the idea that she is in any way

like the dead woman who drank in bars. She refuses to believe
that she resembles previous occupants of the house who have
lived and died shut away behind the privet and the beech.
Chauvin concedes the point but having weakened her by allow-
ing her this small 'rational' success, he attacks again through
her fear where neither reason nor habit protect her. Speak
quickly, he orders: 'Inventez'.

And again Anne must make a considerable effort. As if
controlled by a force outside herself, she speaks of freedom
('ville sans arbres'), screams, violence ('orages') and death
('oiseaux égorgés'). It is a hallucinatory version of her oppressive past and a vision of a possible alternative, a pure
stream of heightened consciousness as daringly written as it is
unexpected. Yet images of oppression are stronger than the
freer future which she sees less clearly and which she reaches
for only by proxy ('à votre place'): Anne has seen the way
ahead but she has yet to feel its inevitability. But before she
can come to terms with her vision, Chauvin without warning
advances a totally new view of the murder: perhaps there were
no long discussions (like their own) but simply a sudden urge
to kill: 'Parlez-moi', he demands (p. 59; 44).

This time, she cannot respond, though it is not fear that
prevents her from speaking but rather the 'joy' of drawing
closer to the dead woman who is at this moment a part of her
own existence. Her liberation is echoed in the cries of the
children who greet the evening as a new dawn, the shouts of
the workmen who are released from their work and the breeze
which blows through her stifling life. But the wind recalls the
encircling privet and Chauvin reminds her that like her
neighbours she closes the windows to shut out the sound of
the free wind in the branches. Anne retreats into alcohol and,
in spite of Chauvin's command to 'say anything' (p. 61; 45),
shelters behind the child who, like the wind in the trees, enables
her to ignore the bars of her cage: through him, gate, beech
and privet are diminished. But Chauvin ruthlessly points out
that the love of her child is not to be compared with the
longing she feels. Of true freedom she knows nothing: 'Jamais
vous n'avez crié' (p. 62; 46).

Anne is exhausted, overcome by a torpor which prevents her from responding to this latest challenge. Chauvin's accusation — and her drunkenness — make her less open to the child and more aware of the distance which must be covered before she reaches her 'safe' life in her house which now seems a long way off. Her habits have been undermined and Chauvin, by playing on her fear, has begun to give her new ones.

V. Two days' respite, however, confirms Anne in a determination to cling to the secure world of habit. She tells the child to do what he is told, for music lessons are important. In the background, the orderly port shows how nature may be tamed while, through a window, a mechanical shovel rears up, threatening retribution for all who rebel whether it be against education or the conventions of bourgeois living. The sea is scarcely visible from Mlle Giraud's room.

But the boy is incapable of compromising. If he tells his teacher what *moderato cantabile* means, it is because he is learning to go through the motions and to make gestures which protect his innocence. For his co-operation is only apparent: his reply is not an answer to the question he has been asked. Anne does not need Mlle Giraud to tell her that 'he does it on purpose', for she senses only too clearly that the child acts out of a profound, unconscious and instinctive need to resist the pressures to which he is subject. 'Ma petite honte, mon trésor', she whispers, her conformism giving way before his revolt. Even when the child obeys he is uncompromised, and the sun is in his hair and in his blue eyes. Anne rejoices in the certainty that one day, inevitably, he will know not the music aggressively taught by Mlle Giraud, but the music which lies within him. The sound of the scales covers the murmur of the sea, but his obedience does not vitiate his freedom as Mlle Giraud's rising anger reveals: his 'pose scolaire' (p. 69; 51) is an indication of how little he gives of himself and a reminder that Anne too is a recalcitrant pupil who recites bourgeois lessons 'scolairement'. Anne rejects the conventional wisdom of forcing education on children and once more Mlle Giraud is shocked by her indulgence. A cipher for wider social and moral pressures, Mlle Giraud forces the child to obey.

But if he plays his scales, it is not because he yields to her pressure but because his frustration has not yet brought him to the point of revolt and, more significantly still, because his mother has asked it. But his co-operation is not what Anne wants: what Mlle Giraud believes to be 'good for the character' destroys freedom. Sensing his mother's mood, the boy rebels. The sun suddenly emerges from the mist and lights the sea, while the breeze stirs in his hair signalling an act of revolt which Anne sees on a more personal level: 'mon amour', she murmurs. Mlle Giraud withdraws from the struggle and then begins again wearily. Though the child co-operates now that he has asserted his independence, he gives little of himself, preferring to 'tenter l'impossible' (p. 72; 53) of surrendering to the life which is occurring on the other side of the window. Anne too makes a gesture: 'faussement repentante', she agrees to accept Mlle Giraud's code, to learn her own scales as it were, by speaking seriously to the boy. But she too is overcome by the temptation of the absolute.

For the music that is in him overpowers her. The sonatina leaves her helplessly open to the love which damns her to the inevitable hell of unrealisable goals. The music is the irresistible sign of unshaped innocence and she is 'submerged' by a boundless apprehension of the absolute. The sonatina drains her in the same way that Chauvin's probings exhaust her powers of resistance. It floats out of the window down to the café where Chauvin takes it over. Even the *patronne* responds to it sympathetically. The music has a life of its own — the child is only accidentally a part of it — and as it reaches its climax the sky is filled with a 'monumental' yet 'fragile' assertion of alternative values (pp. 74-75; 55). The sound of the sea and the noises of the café fill the silence and both beckon to Anne who meekly faces Mlle Giraud's final commonsense words. Out of fear of separation from him, she agrees to make the boy practise but with the same 'mauvaise volonté' that lies behind his promise to learn his scales.

The cranes are still against the sky and there is no menace in them now. Anne is filled with love, but she is still left with a question. How can one grasp the infinite when one has never learnt how? Before her own 'education' is complete, there remain lessons which she has still to learn. Instinctively, she seeks out the only person who can teach her how to play her scales.

VI. At this late hour, the café is full. Anne lingers outside, conscious once more of the proprieties. Chauvin persuades her into the bar by hinting at the promise of summer — that is, of release — in the fading sunset. Overruling her weak protests, he forces her to acknowledge that she too is aware, 'ce soir', that the time of waiting is nearing its end. Once inside, her sensuality wells up in her ('sept nuits', p. 78; 58) and she is afraid. But Chauvin's interest in her son's music reassures her. She retreats into this 'safe' subject but, by a subtle association of ideas, Chauvin steers her from the lessons to another piano and thence to the magnolia, fullblown like her sensuality, which she wore on the evening of the reception, between her 'seins nus'. Anne needs to hear him say that at that moment her being was elsewhere, that her eyes were turned towards the garden and beyond. Yet though he has heightened her desire, she still resists. For her memory does not confirm the image he has evoked, but the wine has begun to work and Chauvin presses her: 'Parlez-moi' (p. 80; 59).

Anne lacks the strength to go on but he tells her that their time grows short. All around them the darkness grows, leaving them in the glow of the 'violent' light of the bar just as they are lit by the violent event which occurred exactly one week before. Even the child is aware of the lateness of the hour which is emphasised by the *patronne,* the disappearance of the customers and the radio which already speaks of the next day. Anne becomes aware of Chauvin's hand next to hers on the table and, submitting to the inevitable, speaks of the child, her sleepless nights and restless voyeurism. For the first time, Chauvin abandons his role as guide and interrogator and now judges her by proffering an insult which we do not hear. Anne flinches. 'Continuez', he orders (p. 81; 60).

She fully realises the nature of her nocturnal restlessness but still clings to the notion that it may be checked by the

routine of her days. But even this certainty now begins to
fade: the piano lessons, conceived as a means of asserting the
primacy of her child in her life, have themselves become part
of the 'heures fixes' which regulate her life and stifle her being.
Now, by accepting that she will be late, she has reached the
point where the safety of routine has become unbearable.
Chauvin waits for the knowledge that revolt is inevitable to
work in her. She grieves, like her son, for the women who
died in her house but Chauvin warns her neither to look back
to false pity nor forward to a falser escape to other seas: the
'je m'en irai' which she pronounced two days before must
mean more than that. But she seems to need no such reminder.
The red knitting grows longer, the waves beat against the
wharf, but for her time has ceased to matter and Chauvin has
no need to prompt her.

What she needs to know is the precise instant when the
man (for she now understands everything about the woman)
knew that she had to die. Chauvin replies that it was probably
at the last moment that he wanted her dead. 'Hypocritically',
Anne speaks of herself under cover of the dead woman through
whom she lives and now hopes to 'die' (p. 84; 62). Chauvin,
who has revealed something of his own involvement by in-
sulting her, adds a confession which Anne understands perfectly.
Murderer and victim shared the same 'hope', but so do Anne
and Chauvin. The time for talking is past; the preliminaries of
estrangement and death may now begin.

When she asks him to talk of the murder — to invent if
necessary, as she herself has invented — his voice is neutral
and quite unfamiliar (p. 85; 63). He outlines the couple's
disintegration which happened 'over a period of days' and
which drove the man to chase the woman away. The woman
always went, though she wished to stay, a situation which
Anne is coming to know only too well. She begs for mercy, as
though they are reliving the drama first acted out by others.
Chauvin continues remorselessly: the intensity of their love
was made tolerable only by habit, but habit obscured the man's
perception of the woman until finally he was unable to see her
as she was and at this moment his fear began. This too is part

of Chauvin's confession for he has become the man as Anne has become the woman. She clings to the child but just as she is 'blinded' so does Chauvin avert his eyes: the time for 'seeing' has not yet come. In turn, Anne relives the woman's actions, an invention which draws a second insult which she accepts in the spirit of the dead woman who accepted humiliation because it was the only form of hope left to her. Chauvin recoils from the dazed expression on Anne's face and again insults her, this time pronouncing the word clearly and signifying his scorn for the lubricious, contemptible creature he now sees before him (p. 87; 64). Anne too recoils, suddenly aware of the distance which separates them. Yet adapting once more to her mood, which has been his role throughout their conversations, he retracts. But the situation is irretrievable. She no longer needs his prompting and her clear perception of the truth makes his denial superfluous: she looks avidly at the 'inhuman' expression on his face and at last sees the hatred and violence that exist between them. For it is Anne who now takes the initiative, forcing the climax, miming hands around her throat, acting out a murder which is also a form of suicide (p. 88; 65). In this moment of madness, she anticipates her 'death' and then lucidity returns. Chauvin, unprepared for the speed of Anne's revolt, dismisses this woman whom he no longer recognises. Like the murderer, he will not see her truly except through an act of murder which, though inevitable, still lies in his future. Anne is led away by her child knowing that 'c'est fini': she is prepared to meet her death which cannot now be long in coming.

VII.   Anne arrives late for the dinner party which presents the bourgeoisie at its devotions. It is a ritual assembly, the affirmation of an orderly world which lives by propriety and decorum but has its being in money and power. The guests have clothed their human nakedness in uniforms which denote standing and success, and they accept unquestioningly the tribute of tradition, the sweat of the cooks and the complicity of the servants. The distance separating this 'univers étincelant' from the natural world outside (the wind, the sea and the garden are never far away) is to be measured by the lifelike but lifeless 'saumon des eaux libres': presented as a triumph of art over nature, it is a ghastly parody of its former beauty and freedom. Yet the elegance of the salmon, the arrival in its time of the duck (another sacrificial dish) and the graciousness of the ceremonies do not entirely obscure the voraciousness of the assembled company: they merely represent the accepted forms into which nature has been forced. In the same way, these women wear the acceptable face of love. To them, Anne will reveal the naked face of passion.

The claims of nature are made in stark counterpoint to the 'moderato' of the dinner. Only Anne, like an animal at bay, resists. Her resistance is numb and far removed from the biting irony which Mme Duras (in an unusually direct satirical vein) injects into the scene. Anne's response is much more instinctive and is expressed through symbolic gestures. The guests see her toy with her food, smile vacantly and drink glass after glass of wine. But the reader notes that she leans against the piano as she once did when receiving Chauvin at another reception; we watch her crumple her magnolia in time to another ritual. For outside, the magnolia tree is in full flower, a 'floraison funèbre' which parallels the fading of the bloom which Anne wears and which she destroys and eventually discards. As time passes relentlessly, the salmon disappears, the moon rises, the duck is consumed and digestion begins — and Anne's flower, symbol of her eroticism, exudes its irresistible perfume and inevitably withers.

She is judged by the servants, by her guests and by her husband, but as her lucidity weakens she passes beyond propriety. She hears only stray remarks, sees only glimpses of an arm or a bare shoulder and withdraws into a contemplative stupor. Consumed by that 'other' hunger, she is carried by the wine beyond 'la déraison' into a near-trance in which she has a clear vision of the garden, sleeping now like her child, and of the sea beyond. Garden, sea, windows, gate, wind, music, trees — the stuff of her conversations with Chauvin — have turned into a private language by means of which she communicates directly with the unnamed watcher outside: the odour of the magnolias brings them mystically together and establishes them in a moment of complete but fleeting intimacy. Anne has no need to see him, for she knows he is there. She has no need of any other contact, for they cannot be closer. So strong is the sensation that her efforts to dissemble simply become 'la grimace désespérée et licencieuse de l'aveu' (p. 99; 73). At a similar moment, the murderer too had lost all dignity and now Anne's eyes, like his, express only her desire. The wine, which tastes of a man's lips, has revealed the true nature of her 'dark desires' but it cannot appease her hunger.

Outside, the man looks at the sea and the garden and stares at his hands. He progresses from a state of *attente* to a *moment* at which he knows what he must do. Urged on by the sea, the wind and the scent of the magnolias, he attempts a direct assault on the gates of Anne's prison but halts, struck by the sudden knowledge of what his hands must do: they will make an end of things. As inevitably as the magnolia will fade, so the desire to kill has come upon the watching man (p. 101; 74).

As the dinner ends, the beach is empty and the magnolia is dead: Anne's summer has ended. At the foot of her son's bed (where he is dreaming still of red motor-boats), in the aura of his innocence, she slowly expels the food she has eaten. It is a clear gesture of rejection, a revolt against the values of her middle-class world. Her husband has nothing to say to her.

VIII.   After the high tensions of the dinner party, the last encounter between Anne and Chauvin begins on a prosaic note. We are informed, as we were at the start of chapter IV, that the unusual fine spell has lasted, though there is now in the air a sense of imminent resolution: in retrospect, the day may be remembered as a turning point. It is by means of such apparent trivialities that Mme Duras hints that the moment of crisis is near.

The scene is familiar and the décor the same — the setting sun, the wind from the sea, the knitting (grown larger and more insistent), the noise of the factory, the barges unloading at the docks — but the atmosphere is charged with new ten-

sions. Neither Anne nor Chauvin seems to notice the other's
appearance, the kindliness of the *patronne* or even their
surroundings, though they look at the weather outside and at
the interior of the café. They have reached such a point of
mutual understanding that they see more than eyes observe
and hear more than their words say. The dialogue falters,
punctuated by silences and burdened by feelings and new intuitions at which we can only guess. If Anne finds it difficult
to agree that she has come alone, it is because her 'yes' (p. 107;
78) is an admission that she has outgrown the need for the
reassuring presence of her child: by it, she indicates that she
has accepted her solitude. Chauvin is wearily resigned to what
must happen and perfunctorily acknowledges this separation
from the child which is also a separation from her bourgeois
life of which the piano lessons had become part. But Anne's
revolt is more comprehensive still and she proceeds to explain
her 'vomissement' as a rejection of the wine through which she
pursued the murdered woman and Chauvin himself. Chauvin's
flat acceptance of this defection draws a cry of anguish from
Anne who, unlike Chauvin who has no more to say, still needs
to explain that her conscious will has no control over the
groundswell of revolt that surges within her. She needs to
explain that she 'invented' her son as an extension of her own
desires, but he refuses to listen. Gradually the initiative passes
to Anne. She fills his glass and persuades him to place his
hand on hers. Their hands already have the coldness of death
and remain in 'leur pose mortuaire' (p. 110; 81). Anne's moans
of anguish and despair are quieted by this symbolic assertion
of their complicity, for the will to die is upon her.

Their time is almost finished and Anne begs Chauvin to
speak one last time of the murder through which she will find
the strength to face her own death. Again they act out the game
of motives, their personal identities weakening as they recreate
the moment. Chauvin's voice is neutral while Anne's face
begins to take on the pallor of death: the identification of
both with the other lovers is complete and as they realise
it both begin to tremble. It is Chauvin who breaks the mood
by admitting that he knows nothing and Anne responds with

sudden decisiveness: 'Elle ne parlera plus jamais' (p. 112; 82). Less bold, Chauvin tells her that nothing is finished, that one day a man or perhaps a child humming a tune will break that silence. But Anne's flat denial is the muted expression of her calm yet lyrical anticipation of imminent release. The siren conspires with her, blowing interminably; the sun's last, wild rays connive at her liberation: the 'allégresse' of the siren and the 'calme gonflement' of the clouds hold out a promise of the *moderato cantabile* which is at last within her reach. But again she falters, suddenly afraid of freedom. Chauvin would snatch her back with a kiss, but it is Anne who consummates their strange affair with a kiss of farewell which is neither *appassionato* nor *patetico* but a kiss of death.

Anne is now alone with her fear and almost 'screams', so intensely is she afraid. She has outgrown her child and her way of life and her contact with Chauvin is almost over. At last, free of constraint, she is alone with her true self which, by accepting her fear, she faces for the first time. A final hesitation: perhaps she lacks the strength to attain the impossible. Chauvin, gentle now or perhaps merely resigned, gives her a moment during which she emerges, solitary and unwatched, as 'cette femme adultère', no longer the respected wife and mother. 'Je voudrais que vous soyez morte', he says. If Chauvin's desire is murderous, it is Anne who translates it into reality: 'c'est fait' (p. 114; 84). It is, in the terms we have come to accept, a deliberate, inevitable death by suicide. Chauvin gestures as if to call her back or perhaps to wave goodbye, but Anne's destiny is decided. Very alone and utterly free, she walks towards the setting sun to find her way in a more harmonious and natural world where we — our ears filled with the sound of the commonsense world — cannot follow her.

* * *

Anne Desbaresdes is a conventional, middle-class wife of ten years' standing. Her conduct has always been blameless and yet, even before she hears the *pure scream* which dislocates her existence, she is dimly aware that her life is oppressive.

She quiets her unease by projecting her longings onto her son in whom she sees the joyful spontaneity which her past and her social position deny her. It is for this reason that, much to Mlle Giraud's dismay, she indulges the boy's rebelliousness. But what is harmless wish-fulfilment assumes a more vital form as the scream rings out and the sight of the murderer sprawled upon his victim implants in her, not a romantic death wish, but a powerful intuition that love can be perfectly realised only in death. Loving limits Love — 'aucun amour au monde ne peut tenir lieu de l'amour' (5, p. 198) — and only when removed from space and time can Love be pure. In the eyes of the murderer, she sees the absolute, other-worldly desire which she will never know as long as she remains what she has become: a conventional *bourgeoise* living a life of routine respectability. What for others is a mere 'fait divers' becomes the *trigger* which releases her inert frustrations. Her long and passive *attente* is interrupted by an unexpected *moment*. In Durassian terms (see chapter 2), Anne has stopped looking and has begun to see.

Moderato cantabile is therefore not so much a love story as the exploration of a crisis. Anne becomes aware of her *ennui* and catches sight of the *impossible*. Her *revolt* is abetted by *nature* and characterised by *imprudence*. Her inner journey is punctuated by *fear* and supported by a groundswell of unconscious *will* which forces her to deny her acquired *identity* and live out *substitute* emotions until she reaches the point where she *destroys* her old self and passes beyond *death* into the pure freedom where Love is total. Anne ceases to be the *voyeur* of the child's innocence or the murderer's desire, for she acquires her own clear vision of the absolute. The emancipation of Anne Desbaresdes could take place nowhere else but in this carefully structured Durassian universe.

Thus if Anne seeks the company of Chauvin, it is not because she is unhappily married — Mme Duras has made a point of saying that her marriage is sexually satisfying (29, p. 60) — but because she needs to talk. She is drawn to Chauvin because he claims to speak authoritatively of the murder. That he knows little more than she does soon ceases to matter, for he knows instinctively what Anne wants to hear: that the murder was executed under the sign of Love. Chauvin is less a retailer of facts than a fellow-conspirator, a fiction-maker who satisfies a need for invention. Through him, she turns vicarious experience into her own reality. She finds him attractive enough for her sensuality to be aroused, but Anne is no Madame Bovary who surrenders to seduction in the hope of reaching a dream. Chauvin externalises her confused emotions and acts as a catalyst for the mysterious reactions taking place within her. As Mme Duras has said, in a Preface written ten years after the publication of *Moderato cantabile* (*24*, pp. 9-10), he is 'un accident secondaire, de nature interchangeable dans la vie de l'héroïne'. In other words, Chauvin happens to be the man from whom Anne hears the story 'qu'elle attendait d'entendre un jour'. Anne sees him as the surest means of access to the love she needs and which he seems to understand so well. 'Ce que veut Anne Desbaresdes de Chauvin c'est ce qu'elle n'a jamais vécu mais c'est ce qu'elle aurait pu vivre avec et à travers d'autres hommes: son anéantissement dans l'amour même'. Elsewhere, Mme Duras further suggests that Anne is drawn to him because 'ce qu'elle devine en lui, c'est une disposition au meurtre... Il a vu le crime se faire. Et il l'a interprété comme elle le voulait. Il a raconté un mensonge pour lui plaire. Elle sait que c'est un mensonge. Mais qu'il ait deviné si bien ce qu'elle voulait, en fait un complice admirable' (*1*, p. 67). Chauvin does not merely provide an opportunity for a passing affair: through him, Anne lives Love itself and lives it unto death. For her 'adultery' is total. Her quest is for completeness and self-knowledge. She seeks the end of her acquired identity, of her role as wife and mother, of her bourgeois self. As she leaves the café for the last time, she knows who and what she is. What use she can make of this knowledge belongs to another story which lies in the future, though Mme Duras has suggested 'qu'elle marchera probablement vers la folie' (*1*, p. 68).

Mme Duras's scattered comments are illuminating, for they confirm the reader's impression that *Moderato cantabile* is not an *histoire d'amour,* or even much of a story, but a fable of a woman who loses the world and gains herself. It cannot be taken as an example of realistic fiction, for there is neither plot nor character in the conventional sense. Mme Duras drops a pebble into a pool: we see the ripples but not their source. She invites us to work outward from the point of impact much as a scientist may seek to reconstruct, from the aftermath of an explosion, the event that is the birth or death of a star. 'Ce qui m'intéresse dans une situation romanesque, c'est son ombre ou celle qu'elle projette sur les êtres alentour. Chacun de mes romans se présente comme un négatif [où les lecteurs], s'ils sont de bonne volonté, doivent s'y retrouver et remplir les vides que je laisse dans mes livres' (*28*, p. 4). In interviews she has given, Mme Duras fills in the odd 'blanc': Anne's marriage is happy, she will become mad, the unnamed town is 'un petit port de la Manche' (*27*, p. 68). But what interests her more than such 'facts' which were available to her imagination, is the presentation of an 'expérience intérieure'. 'La seule chose qui me passionne, c'est rendre compte d'une situation intérieure. Je pense que le reste a été fait. C'est ce que nous avons essayé dans *Moderato cantabile*' (*29*, p. 60). She has admitted that the novel is as autobiographical as *Un Barrage contre le Pacifique*. It emerged from 'une histoire sexuelle' (*17*, pp. 59-60) which, incidentally, also surfaces in *L'Homme assis dans le couloir* (1980) which is the definitive text of a short story composed in 1959 and a kind of *Moderato cantabile* stripped of anecdote. But Mme Duras makes clear that it is a personal experience discreetly robbed of its actuality: 'il n'y a rien de visible qui vienne de moi' (*34*, p. 92). An abstract of private emotions which are offered up for reconstruction by the reader, *Moderato cantabile* 'n'est pas écrit comme un roman. Ça veut plutôt être un poème' (*31*, pp. 654-5).

In choosing to explore the 'expérience intérieure', Mme Duras was conscious that she was breaking new ground. For her purpose was not to be achieved by reliance on the well-worn techniques of realistic fiction. 'Ce que je recherche avant tout,' she stated in 1959, 'c'est à désencombrer la littérature du bavardage romanesque' (*28*, p. 1). Writers who leave nothing unsaid (like Hugo, for instance, who lacks the quality

Mme Duras most admires, that of 'laconisme') leave nothing for the reader to do, deny his imagination and turn him into a passive spectator. Mme Duras is less concerned with having willing followers than active readers. If *Moderato cantabile* has an impact, it is not because the message is new but because our active participation turns Anne's quest into part of our experience, reconstitutes it as dramatically as boiling water on powdered potato. After all, *Romeo and Juliet* demonstrates that love is perfect only in death, and countless authors have told us that bourgeois values dull the soul, that pure innocence is found only in childhood, that mere sensual gratification brings disillusion and that freedom is the highest good. Marguerite Duras reactivates the eternal verities in her own personal, 'poetic' terms. But if, like all works of art, *Moderato cantabile* is a work of persuasion and propaganda, it succeeds precisely because it does not state ideas but shows them. Written over a period of four months and revised in a mood of intense empathy — 'un état second', in Mme Duras's own words — *Moderato cantabile* is a strange and disturbing tale whose haunting power testifies to its creator's great originality and considerable artistry.

4

The Art of *Moderato cantabile*

THE 'plot' of *Moderato cantabile* is quickly summarised — two people discuss a murder — but a simple résumé is not much help in enabling us to come to terms with the book. Indeed, apart from the arrest of the murderer, nothing happens which a reader of traditional fiction would call 'action'. Nor is such a reader given much of a lead in his efforts to understand why the characters act, or rather react, as they do. He does not know what they look like nor is he told about the events which have precipitated the crisis which develops. He searches in vain for the usual narrative and psychological pointers and is forced to listen to boats chugging outside windows, to watch suns setting over seas and to decode significant glances and trivial statements. The laws of cause and effect are not suspended exactly, but causes are elusive and their effects are puzzling. It is as though what is peripheral in most novels has been thrust into the very centre of *Moderato cantabile* which, at first reading, seems unspecific and diffuse. Yet from the start there is an undeniable tension, a constant sense of something about to happen. Though nothing in the conventional sense actually happens — Chauvin does not strangle Anne, for instance, nor does her husband intervene — we do not feel cheated. There is suspense enough to satisfy our need for 'story'.

Mme Duras's determination to eliminate 'le bavardage romanesque' — the novelist's habit of telling all there is to know about his characters and of explaining how their past, psychology and actions illuminate their predicament — is therefore very evident. Indeed, the third-person narrator seems often to know no more than the average spectator. It is not certain that Mlle Giraud is aware of the boy's innocence as he scratches his leg, nor can the story-teller confirm that the murderer weeps as he is driven away. Conversations are minuted but remain opaque; looks and gestures are noted but not explained; the position of the sun and the sound of the siren are recorded but not interpreted. Mme Duras's whole stance as a narrator invites us to supply missing links. If the traditional novelist tells a story, she shows it happening through such apparently random notations. It is in this sense that *Moderato cantabile* is a drama in which the reader is forced into the role of participant. But it is an interior drama which, apart from a few gestures and surprised reactions, is rarely allowed to surface. Anne's progress from *ennui* to revolt is implied, not stated, and Mme Duras's art is the art of indirect and oblique suggestion.

But if the 'plot' of *Moderato* is elusive, so are the protagonists. From the few hints we are given about Anne's past, it would appear that her behaviour contradicts her character. Normally sober and respectable, she drinks more than is good for her and behaves in a manner which shocks the patrons of the bar almost as much as it does her husband and his circle. Mlle Giraud is a nicely observed study of a disillusioned piano-teacher, but we hear no more of her once she has served her purpose. The child too is neatly captured with a few touches but, like Anne's husband or the *patronne,* plays a patently functional role. Most perplexing of all, however, is Chauvin who seems decidedly too acute and too articulate to be the unemployed workman he is said to be. Like Anne, we know little of him except what he says and does, but we are left wondering if he is a real person at all. At times, his sexual interest in Anne is explicit. Yet the seducer in him inevitably gives way to the interrogator who uses the sexual interest he has aroused as a weapon against her refusal to face up to what she is. Thus Chauvin, the 'emancipated' workman, is by turn tempter, seducer and, at times, almost a psychoanalyst. For there are moments when their conversation takes on a clinical aspect as Chauvin leads Anne closer to self-knowledge. Yet Chauvin, the therapeutic analyst, emerges as an actor in the drama: he too is involved in Anne's quest and yet remains the instrument by which she finally achieves her freedom.

Yet we can say that Anne is inconsistent, that the background characters are functional and that Chauvin plays several conflicting roles, only if we insist on treating the novel as a work of realism. Anne and Chauvin might inhabit a world of their own, but their actions and gestures are described conventionally enough. The naturalness of the boy, the music lessons (horribly familiar to anyone who has tried to learn the piano), the bustle of the café, even the occasional information about what the 'ordinary' townspeople are saying about the weather — are all recognisably 'real'. Behind Anne and Chauvin, we glimpse the conventional life of the town, the factories and the Desbaresdes's social circle. Yet the conspiring sunsets, the geography of Anne's house and its gloomy garden, or the marvellously impressionistic account of the dinner party all seem to exude meanings just as the conversations imply far more than they say. For there is little here that may be taken at face value: the boy's very naturalness is a sign of his spontaneous innocence, the music lessons are a cipher for oppression while the prosaic life of the bar and the town provides a measure of the distance which separates Anne from our world. It is by, at most, semi-realistic evocations that Mme Duras manages to convey inner states and sudden intuitive shifts. Just as an apparently banal remark may draw a strangely intense reaction, so the apparent realism of *Moderato cantabile* creates its deeper meanings.

But the novel is not merely semi-realistic: it is semi-theatrical. Its three interior 'sets' (Mlle Giraud's room, the café and Anne's house) establish a mood of claustrophobia which occasional glimpses of the sky (through a window usually) or Anne's return journeys along the increasingly unreal Boulevard de la Mer only serve to heighten. The manner in which the story is presented is itself theatrical, even cinematographic. During its eight 'scenes', the narrator at times does little more than supply stage directions to the dialogue, which bears the burden of advancing the narrative. Remarks are exchanged and their significance is heightened by a reference to hands or the

sun. Indeed, Anne's quest becomes clearer if we see her in
theatrical terms: as wife and mother, she has been miscast
and her struggle to find a new role reaches a climax in the
dinner scene when she shows 'le faciès impudique de l'aveu',
concedes that she can no longer sustain the part society requires
her to play and finally drops her mask. But we can take the
theatrical metaphor even further. Much of the dialogue belongs
to a far subtler 'inner theatre' which shows Anne and Chauvin
acting out the murder they have 'created'. Their meetings
become part of a 'play-within-a-story' and their conversations
assume a role-playing character which externalises their identification with the assassin and his dead mistress. The whole
process takes place against a background of ritual, another
form of theatre which Mme Duras establishes very deliberately.
The music lesson and the dinner are formal rites which demand
reverence and respect. They display the power of the world
which requires the individual to accept agreed patterns of
conformity. Anne's attitude to Mlle Giraud and her guests
indicates that she is ready to respond to other rites which
enshrine alternative values. But more is involved than the
replacement of one set of rituals by another. Through the
quickly established 'cérémonial' of her encounters with Chauvin, the 'floraison funèbre' of the magnolias which signals the
end of her affair and the 'rite mortuaire' which suggests the
imminence of separation and 'death', Anne reaches the point
at which she no longer needs to play a role or pay ritual
tribute to forces that lie outside her. She is no longer under
any obligation to 'act': she is strong enough to be herself.
When she finally leaves the café, she also leaves her artificial,
theatrical life and enters a more profoundly real world.

But ritual is exploited not merely for its theatrical value.
It constitutes one of the many symbolic strands which bind
the book together and define the nature and progress of Anne's
quest. *Moderato cantabile* jangles with symbols like the man-
nequin whose pocket Gringoire tries to pick in Hugo's *Notre
Dame*. For example, Mme Duras keeps us well informed about
the weather: the whole town talks of it, the radio broadcasts
the meteorological report, and the strength of the wind, the

position of the sun, the arrival of evening are recorded so insistently that more than realism or the conventional 'pathetic fallacy' seems to be implied. The unusual fine spell not only frames the book but is a suspension of the normal, a lull which nature offers Anne as an opportunity to break with her past. In the 'premières chaleurs' of this 'printemps précoce' lies a promise of the high summer of her liberation, and for as long as the good weather lasts the elements conspire with her. The cool wind blows away the threatening man-made clouds and writes messages of 'autres voies' against the evening sky. The breeze punctures the 'stifling' atmosphere in which Anne 'suffocates', but it is the sun which shows her the way most persistently. It lights the boy's head and fills his mouth, consecrating his innocence as later it transfers its benediction to Chauvin. It glows most redly as the scream rings out and at moments when Anne draws nearer to Chauvin, even throwing 'leurs ombres conjuguées' onto the café wall as if it would hasten their union. When Anne finally leaves the bar, bathed 'dans la lumière rouge qui marquait le terme de ce jour-là', we understand that she has finally answered a call which has grown more and more insistent. Her emancipation is actively willed by nature.

Yet it is not only the weather which connives at her release. The sea intrudes constantly, now retreating respectfully before the clarion call that is the dying woman's scream, now returning relentlessly to fill silences and undermine Anne's resistance with its promise of 'eaux libres'. Yet though courteous and discreet, nature does not beckon benignly: it commands and makes her afraid. She knows that the wind, when it wishes, can smash the windows which divide her imprisoned self from the dangerous world of freedom; she has seen the sea so angry that it cripples sea-gulls and prevents children sleeping. She is aware of the threat that lies in the beech tree which hides the sea, its shadow black as ink; she feels the attraction of the magnolia, but knows that 'on peut en rêver et en être malade tout le jour qui suit'. For if she aspires to Love, she senses that love and violence are inseparable and it is through the intolerant, uncompromising natural world that we share her fear.

Each of her senses is systematically attacked: she sees and hears nature's moods, smells the sea and the magnolia, tastes the wine which savours of a man's kiss and touches his cold hand and deathly lips. It is through the 'other hunger' of her eroticism that Anne enters more and more into harmony with this natural world of beauty and savagery. And it is through Mme Duras's calculated use of natural symbolism that we grow closer to Anne's obsessive mood.

The natural world is thus used to illuminate an 'expérience intérieure' which, in terms of action and psychology, remains invisible. But it is also used to provide the 'inner drama' with its basic structure. For instance, Chauvin turns the magnolia, 'imprisoned' behind the Desbaresdes's gate, into a symbol of Anne's repressed sensuality. By insisting upon the flower and its associations, he reveals Anne's true nature to her. At the dinner party, she leans against the piano and wears a magnolia as though to re-enact the reception where she met Chauvin for the first time. But the inevitable fading of the flower anticipates the death of her desire for Chauvin: once she shut her window against it, but now she is accustomed to its heady scent. In other words, by drawing our attention periodically to the magnolia, Mme Duras enables us to reconstruct Anne's slow awakening and to understand why her last meeting with Chauvin is totally devoid of sensuality. If we find it difficult to see Anne directly, she is clearly reflected in the large number of structural symbols which litter the text.

The group house-garden-gates-hedge-window-blind renders her 'imprisoned' life very effectively just as the café, situated between the land and the sea but also between her 'bourgeois' house and the 'proletarian' town, is defined as a 'lieu indécis' where an act of Durassian liberation is most likely to occur. The 'vedette' seen through Mlle Giraud's window symbolises freedom and subsequently reappears at varying levels of intensity as the tug-boats which come and go and the red motor-boat of which the boy still dreams in chapter VII. The theme of innocence surfaces periodically through the child, but also in Chauvin's 'yeux d'enfant', Anne's 'voix enfantine' and the children who sleep or are prevented from sleeping. Comparable symbolic chains link the 'milky' hands which play the piano to the hands which will commit murder, while the 'regard absent' of the assassin is father to a whole series of looks and glances which culminate in Anne's final unwatched solitude. As she drifts towards the 'délire' of the murderer, she is summoned to return by variants of 'raisonnable' and 'lucide' which indicate that her 'déraison' is to be preferred to her 'sanity'. The dying woman's scream recurs in her memory of childbirth, the seagulls which screech 'comme des égorgés' and in the 'cria presque Anne Desbaresdes' of the final chapter which reveals how close she is to death by Chauvin's hand.

In a sense, the scream is a key sound which gives rise to all kinds of 'appels raisonnables', 'rumeurs de la foule' and 'cris d'hommes' which bring the story sonorously to life. But there are other sounds which have specific functions. The siren, which is a regular reminder of the urgency of the drama; the sonatina, which is variously a sign of the boy's defeat or of his emancipation and emerges ultimately as a pure expression of the inexpressible; the radio, which signals the existence of the prosaic world and acts as a counterweight to Anne's reverie. But if there are key-sounds, there are also master colours. The sunsets, the blood, the wine, the *patronne*'s knitting, the motor-boat, the 'nuages incendiés', even the copper beech, are red or pink or ochre, the colour of passion and death. Curtains and blinds are white and eyeless — unlike Anne, Chauvin and the boy who all have those blue eyes which, for Mme Duras, are bottomless and unfathomable like the sky (*17,* pp. 12-13). But the white of the magnolia is funereal just as the black of the police-van, the shadow of the beech or the night of the dinner-party evokes menace and death. Both sounds and colours are carefully orchestrated and, like so many of Mme Duras's recurring symbols, provide a subtle commentary on the action and serve as a means of access to the drama which unfolds.

As Anne, at the dinner party, communicates with the watcher outside by means of a private, non-verbal language (magnolia, sea, gates, etc.), so the reader becomes party to the novel by reading the many symbols which chart her progress. Anne may seem elusive and her obsession may appear difficult to grasp. But gradually her image acquires substance as she is passed through a hall of mirrors which reflect her past, her present and her future. If what is peripheral to most novels seems to occupy the very centre of *Moderato cantabile,* it is because the centre becomes visible by inference: upon Anne and her goal are focussed the colours, the sounds, the whole range of symbolic values which give her definition and clarity.

The novel's randomness is therefore deceptive. Plot and character may be noticeable by their absence, but they are replaced by other patterns which control and direct our response. For the symbols are rarely inert: they have life and movement which mobilise the apparent stasis of the central situation. A symbol may even have the character and function of an event. The series 'piano-magnolia' not only expresses Anne's sensuality but is the matrix of her conduct at the dinner party: she behaves now as she should have behaved a year previously at the reception. Other symbolic series have structural duties. The setting of the sun and the arrival of evening are constant indications that everything runs its course: the music lesson must end, the salmon must 'ineluctably' disappear, even the last day arrives at its 'terme'. It is thus that the palpable sense of inevitability which hangs over Anne's encounters with Chauvin is made into a dramatic and incontrovertible reality. There is no fate or destiny beyond the natural order which decrees that nothing remains the same: 'l'implacable précision du hasard' (pp. 54-55; 40-41) is no less implacable or unavoidable for being an effect of chance. Such constant reminders of the inevitability of all things create a tension of which Anne and Chauvin are all too aware. Anne is stirred to the depths of her being by the scream but is both unable and unwilling to move beyond her intuition of the absolute to a stage where she will act as she now feels. Her need to talk is stronger than the desire to become, but she is not allowed the luxury of procrastination. When she is with Chauvin, the present fades as they live through the 'dead' couple and emerge into a timeless world where truth is bright and clear and where what they seem to remember is the only reality. At such moments, they cease to see each other clearly, the café recedes and they are bathed in the lurid after-glow of the instant of love and death. They invent a new calendar which dates from that instant ('Il y a maintenant trois jours... sept jours — Sept nuits... Ça va être la huitième nuit') which not only traces Anne's progress from respectability to eroticism but also places them outside real time. Incapsulated by nostalgia for a remembered experience which they have neither observed nor shared but invented, they move backwards and forwards through space and time. Yet the recurring symbols of sunsets, sirens and the arrival of the workmen constantly jerk them back to the 'fixed hours' of clock time and generate a sense of urgency, of time running out, which is at the heart of the suspense the reader feels. Each meeting moves them forward, as though it would break the tension, yet each time Anne leaves Chauvin with nothing resolved. It is against this pattern of repeated anti-climax that the final chapter, the most understated in the book, is dominated by an electric sense of endlessly postponed, tumescent inevitability. It takes Anne only one minute to jettison all that restrains her, but it is a minute which has been carefully prepared by an artful seeding of symbols.

The crisis in Anne's life exists in an existential void which is given its shape and its peculiarly dense texture by such inferences and associations. But if her progress is charted by reference to external values, the space it occupies lies in the interstices between other lives: she inhabits an unreal world which lies at the confluence of other worlds. We see little of Mlle Giraud, for instance, and less of Monsieur Desbaresdes, but we cannot help making assumptions about both of them. Each predicates a 'récit absent', a *mise en abyme,* through which we define Anne's image. But the most striking example of the 'récit absent' is obviously the *crime passionnel* about which we know very little. Anne and Chauvin seem to wish to reconstruct the murder, yet neither is concerned with mere facts. Anne brushes aside the banal contribution of the *patronne* ('mariée..., trois enfants, et ivrogne') and Chauvin's language betrays his purpose: he moves from 'savoir' to 'croire' and finally to 'imaginer'. Rather they invent the murder, identify with its mood and *become* the victim and her killer. We pass beyond inference and association and are confronted by an example of direct substitution. As they substitute themselves for these other selves, we see the truth they seek re-staged against the background of the other story whose outcome we know. We may anticipate that their relationship will follow the same, inevitable pattern from love through talk to frustration, violence and death. The 'récit absent' not only externalises the 'situation intérieure' but provides the novel with a basic linear structure. But since Anne's emancipation is sandwiched between the 'récit absent' of the murder and the unwritten 'histoire inexistante' of her subsequent life, we can add that *Moderato cantabile* is also perfectly circular. When we observe Anne leave the bar for the last time, we are returned to the point at which we first saw the murderer.

Symbols which are so many structural devices, the linear thrust which leads us from love to death, the circular movement from a real to a substitute murder, the upward spiral of the sense of inevitability — *Moderato cantabile* is an exceptionally intricate novel. Yet structurally the book is far more complex than even this suggests. The framework is simple enough: two music lessons, five encounters and a dinner occupy ten days in a meticulously noted linear progression. Yet, as we have seen, time for the characters strays from the clock, moving backwards and forwards so insistently that onto surface chronology is superimposed a no less carefully structured inner time. Within this contrapuntal framework, each chapter begins slowly, moves dramatically forward and ends in bathos. All the conversations, save the last, start with Anne's arrival, continue with the discussion and close with Anne alone with her son. Each encounter is framed by the setting sun and is punctuated by the same references to the *patronne*'s knitting or the inevitable siren. Even the dinner moves forward in time to the 'floraison funèbre' outside and the rhythm of the meal inside. Such carefully arranged structures subtly underscore and illuminate the novel's central themes. The first music lesson, for instance, starts oppressively, reaches a violent climax of instinctive action and ends with a clear reminder of the qual-

itative difference separating 'moderate' conformity from 'lyrical'
desires: 'c'est facile', Anne tells the boy. Recurring articulations
of this kind, together with the repetition of gestures (Anne's
attempts to smooth her dishevelled hair in chapter VII, for
instance) and words (like Chauvin's 'Parlez-moi'), create multiple reverberations to the point where the book's structural
devices interlock so completely that wherever we start we are
led into a complex network of associations.

Yet it is the great strength of *Moderato cantabile* that the
many thematic and structural patterns ultimately settle around
a single organising principle. Critics have many times suggested
that the book is basically a theme with variations. The title
invites such musical metaphors. But as we have suggested, the
title also points to a tension between moderation and lyricism
and it is upon this dialectical pattern that both themes and
structures are arranged. It sets Anne's repressed life against
the repossession of herself; her past against her future; her
sobriety against her drunkenness; her prudence against the
violence of love and death: in Freudian terms, it undermines
her control of the Super Ego and releases the instinctive Ego
of her being. But in a more general sense, it pits the urban
against the natural; real time against a more liberating inner
time; sanity against madness; bourgeois values against non-
conformity. It is only when Anne responds to the 'calme
gonflement' of the clouds that she finally resolves the tension
and moves on in a mood of measured rapture, of understated
certainty.

So deep does the dialectic run that even Mme Duras's art
exists on two distinct but complementary levels: in the story-
teller's voice and in the dialogue which alone carries the
narrative forward. A Duras dialogue replaces 'action': the 'expérience intérieure' is slowly revealed and developed through
what the characters say (or do not say) rather than through
what they do. On the surface, they seem to speak naturally
enough, yet their words provide our sole means of access to
their inner life. In Chapter I, after the murder, the boy asks
'Qu'est-ce que c'est?' to which Mlle Giraud replies 'Recom-
mence!' and Anne adds 'Jamais je ne lui chante des chansons'

(p. 15; 11). None of these statements is part of an exchange of views, for each speaker is shown to be locked in his or her private, non-communicating world — the boy in his innocent curiosity, Mlle Giraud in her respect for discipline and Anne in her foolish egocentricity. There are few exchanges in the book which are not charged with a strange, emotional intensity which is the stronger for not always being clear. Chauvin's first words ('C'était un crime') state merely what is obvious and Anne's reply ('Je me le demandais', p. 25; 18) seems little more than a cover for her embarrassment. Yet his banal remark is really the answer to the question which Anne has just begun to ask herself. Nearly all of Chauvin's lines start multiple resonances of this sort, and this explains why Anne so often struggles to follow where he leads. When she enters the café for the last time, we are told that the child is not with her. The opening dialogue ('Vous êtes seule' — 'Oui', p. 107; 78) appears to re-state the obvious. In fact, Chauvin is acutely aware of the meaning of the child's absence and indirectly invites Anne to acknowledge its significance. She considers his statement carefully, attempts to evade his real question, is at length forced to reply and marvels at her new-found inability to dissemble. Her simple 'Yes' is an enormous admission and its very simplicity 'stifles' her. We are not told why Anne reacts so strangely and she goes on to speak of the weather before returning, several twists of the conversation further on, to the subject: someone else will escort the boy. It is only at this point that we realise that she no longer needs to be propped up by her child, though her phrasing ('C'est une chose que j'ai acceptée...') makes it clear that, though the change was forced on her, the knowledge that she is independent of the boy has dawned as she has been speaking.

Very little of what Mme Duras puts into her characters' mouths thus means simply what it says. Her supercharged, sinewy dialogue is a demanding but marvellously revealing dramatic instrument. Anne in particular is driven to express in words what she is barely aware of feeling and is frequently reduced to inarticulate half-questions, unfinished statements and eloquent silences. She and Chauvin, communicating far below the surface of their words, share a muted garrulousness beneath which we hear them struggling towards a non-verbal certainty which will dispense them from saying anything at all. When Anne announces that 'elle ne parlera plus' (p. 112; 82), we can be sure that like the dead woman she too is nearing total knowledge of herself.

But if Anne struggles for words, Mme Duras is totally in command of her style. Her third-person narrator remains at a distance and her 'peut-être', 'apparemment' and 'comme au hasard' are disconcerting until we realise that the process is perfectly attuned to the business of focussing our attention upon the slowly emerging drama which our questions help to unravel. Her characters are planted in a setting which we ourselves must invent from code-words like 'café', 'salon', 'jardin', 'usine': the décor is suggested, not described, and it is for us to distinguish foreground from background and generally to establish the necessary perspective. In the same way, the people who move across her pages are barely rescued from anonymity. In chapter I, we meet 'la dame', 'l'enfant' and 'une femme' but only the last is identified. Some characters remain nameless (the child, the *patronne*) and others stay faceless (the guests, the workers, Anne's husband, even the solitary watching man). It is a tendency which reaches its limits in chapter VII where 'un homme' now means Monsieur Desbaresdes, now the man outside, and where vague individualities emerge from the undifferentiated 'on'. It is a process which is echoed at the most basic level of style where sudden clarities surge out of the flat monotone of the narrator's voice. This voice reverts consistently to noun and verb at the expense of other parts of speech. It is thus that adjectives of colour or the occasional adverb ('joyeusement', for example, pp. 13, 15; 9, 11) acquire startling relief. Even recurring verbs ('s'étonner', for instance) and nouns (like 'rien') and not least the adjective 'autre' (as in 'd'autre faim' or 'd'autre vin', a somewhat unusual usage which heightens the central notion of 'otherness') may take on an opaque, obsessive quality which gives Mme Duras's style its particular depth. In the same way, departures from the past historic tense, the narrative tense, subtly suggest changes of mood: we enter the new time which is all the more real for not being formally defined. The most successful of the many tense changes is to be found in chapter VII which is written in the present — an immediate but eternal now, the now too of the reader — but ends in the future which affords another indication of the inevitability of Anne's liberation. But time may be dislocated within the same paragraph or even the same sentence. The man outside Anne's house prowls restlessly: 'puis il est revenu, il a redescendu le talus, il est redescendu jusqu'à la grève' (p. 96; 71). Between each verb, time has elapsed and from the *action* of descending we pass to an awareness of his *state* of being down. Sometimes the effect is to slow the action ('L'homme passera outre au parc tôt ou tard. Il est passé' p. 102; 75) but it is more likely to inject an unreal, dreamlike quality into a critical moment. When we read, in Chapter III that Anne 'se leva, se leva avec lenteur, fut levée' (p. 48; 35), what we visualise is a series of still photographs each charged with emotion, each fixing a moment of her anguish, each wrenching her from her spatio-temporal setting and thrusting her into a heightened state of being. Mme Duras's reluctance to use the connecting 'and' ('Il commanda du vin, fit encore un pas vers elle', 'Ils reconnurent cette femme au comptoir, s'étonnèrent', etc.) similarly highlights actions and reactions and creates a mood of incompleteness which shows the workings of 'la théorie des blancs'. What is omitted — from the 'récit absent' to the 'and' of her elegantly asymmetrical sentences — serves to reinforce what is included.

For all its originality, Mme Duras's style is uncluttered and simple. Thus while there are many symbols, there are relatively few images and the images that are used serve to reinforce the symbolism. The role of nature is enhanced by a series of basic similes (e.g., 'têtu comme une chèvre') which tend to centre upon Anne as an animal at bay ('comme dans le guet', 'une bête', 'une bête à la forêt') or which show the power of the forces which threaten her: the steam shovel raises 'ses dents de bête affamée sur sa proie'. Another important series personifies nature (the evening 'balayait la mer', the wind 'tenait le ciel en haleine' and the breeze 'fit frémir l'herbe des cheveux de cet enfant') and underwrites the eventual victory of the living elements. The child's hands are 'milky' and half-opened, like a flower, while the 'honey' of the music he plays is borne like a feather and makes him a tangible part of the harmonious natural world. Anne's vulnerability is suggested by liquid images ('Son image chavirait', she is 'submerged' by the music as she responds to the sea's call) whereas what oppresses her takes on a solid form: the imprisoning garden is 'lisse comme un miroir', the shadow of the beech is 'comme de l'encre noir', the privet creaks 'comme de l'acier' and Chauvin's hand becomes as unresponsive as lead. There are images of violence and ritual death ('comme des égorgés', 'supplicier cette fleur', 'linceul d'oranges', 'pose mortuaire') but also of sacrifice, damnation and the 'portes de l'enfer' which open to Anne the unrepentant. Her crisis is lit from without by images which are as powerful as they are simple.

In *Moderato cantabile,* Mme Duras's control of her material is total. Her art is the art of the half-suggested and the indirect. She does not set out to tell a story but to explore and illuminate a situation. And if her purpose is innovatory, so are her means. Action is replaced by dialogue and the function which 'plot' and 'character' have in traditional fiction is replaced by 'pattern'. Anne's 'expérience intérieure' receives its shape and significance from the obsessive repetition of symbolic and structural motifs, from patterns of colour and sound, gestures, words and images. Indeed the repetition is so insistent that it rises to the level of incantation and imparts an unreal, mythical quality to this strange little tale. Yet the mood remains restrained, for the extensive use of contrast and counterpoint constantly returns the reader to a point of vantage where both poles of the Durassian dialectic are plainly visible. Thus the novel, in spite of its lyricism, remains moderate and subdued in tone. The very strength of feeling is highlighted by Mme Duras's matter-of-factness. If her novel deals with crime, revolt and the most violent emotions, its surface remains calm and unruffled. Passionate yet understated, *Moderato cantabile* itself achieves the balance which is promised in its title.

5

A Note on the Film

SHORTLY after the publication of *Moderato cantabile,* Mme Duras was approached by Alain Resnais with a view to turning her novel into a film. The proposed collaboration ended instead with *Hiroshima mon amour* which won the International Critics' Prize at the Cannes Film Festival in 1959. It was Mme Duras's first venture into the cinema, though René Clément had turned *Un Barrage contre le Pacifique* into a rather 'commercial' film in 1957. Subsequently, other films based on her work by directors like Jules Dassin (*Dix heures et demie du soir en été*) and Tony Richardson (*Le Marin de Gibraltar*) proved equally unsatisfactory and in 1967 Mme Duras began to direct her own films. Since 1971, she has given up writing novels to concentrate on films, where she believes her impact is stronger and her audience wider.

The film of *Moderato cantabile,* directed in 1960 by Peter Brook, was adapted by Mme Duras in collaboration with Gérard Jarlot. As co-author, she was well placed to retain as much of her view-point as was consistent with transferring her original conception to another medium, though what appeared on the screen was ultimately the responsibility of the director. The film had a strong cast in Jean-Paul Belmondo and Jeanne Moreau (whose performance earned her the Best Actress award at Cannes in 1960) and it has become a minor classic in its own right. It is frequently shown and invites comparison with the novel which it both complements and betrays.

The script follows the main structural features of the book: the reader will recognise the two music lessons, the formal dinner and the five conversations even down to small points of dialogue. However, the lines of the novel are blurred by the addition of several new scenes and by significant changes of tone in those which remain. For instance, the second and third conversations occur outside the café (one in an abandoned house reached by ferry, the other in a park) so that the claustrophobic atmosphere and the role of Anne's drinking are considerably reduced. In a new scene placed immediately after the murder, Anne's relationship with her husband is stated much more categorically: a few formal remarks over dinner establish Anne's background and reinforce her perverse admiration for the 'mauvaise volonté' of her son who, we learn, is named Pierre. Two additional scenes on the ferry boat express her indulgent fascination with the boy who, however, during a walk in the Forêt d'Arcy, begins to assert his independence. Alone with her son among the trees, Anne invents a story about deer from a distant land which pass through on their way to a 'far-off country', Germany perhaps. It is a tale which she has often told the boy who is sorry for the deer and suspects the truth — that they are caught and killed. Escaping from her control for the first time, he accuses Anne of making the story up and, in a gesture of revolt against her overprotectiveness, runs off. This new scene suggests that 'Pierre' is growing away from his mother who must seek to fill the void he will leave in her life. Anne's special relationship with her son is thus on the way to becoming a more conventional version of mother-love.

Chauvin too undergoes a subtle transformation. His status is changed — here he is no longer unemployed and 'free' but has a job at the Usines Desbaresdes — and he is seen to show an interest in Anne even before she returns to the café for the first time. Though his sexual interest in her is thus more clearly stated, he remains the inquisitor who leads Anne to self-discovery. Yet it is also suggested that he is closer to the murderer than in the book. In a new scene which follows their second conversation, Chauvin witnesses a police reconstruction of the crime in the café. It is in fact a literal re-enactment of the murder and the assassin gazes into Chauvin's eyes as though to transfer the murderous intent of absolute desire. It is a slightly melodramatic moment designed to point up the parallel between the *crime passionnel* and the symbolic murder which is yet to come. But it also fixes in our memories the exact position of the woman on the floor of the café. When, after the dinner, Anne vomits the 'nourriture étrangère' she has eaten, she adopts precisely the same pose on the floor of the boy's bedroom: her identification with the dead woman is made strikingly clear. To her husband, who asks what he should tell the guests, she does not mumble an excuse but answers: 'Que je suis devenue folle'. It is a far more explicit indication of Anne's 'madness' than is provided by the novel.

The final meeting between Anne and Chauvin occurs in the darkened café immediately after the dinner. It is a move which gains in dramatic tension what it loses in subtlety. Indeed, the overall effect is to dislocate Mme Duras's original intention. By showing Anne seeking out Chauvin at a rendez-vous which he does not want, the film suggests that what is 'impossible' is not Love itself but the banal affair which both would like but which is now out of the question for practical and social reasons. Anne goes so far as to say 'Je crois que je vous aime', though it is clear in the novel that Chauvin is no more than a peg on which she hangs much larger aspirations. However, Chauvin's 'Je voudrais que vous soyez morte' is greeted by a little cry from Anne: 'C'est fait'. But it is he who leaves and Anne, alone in the gloomy café, utters a longer scream which is the scream we heard at the beginning of the film through Mlle Giraud's window: again, the identification is made much more clearly. Anne recovers and leaves the café to join her husband who has driven in search of her and who will presumably take her back to her house and her life from which there will be no escape. Thus she emerges confirmed in her chains, whereas the book sends her off into the symbolic sunset of her new freedom.

In other words, the poetic dimension of the novel is diminished by a combination of Peter Brook's realistic treatment and the actors' naturalistic performances. Chauvin emerges as a tepid seducer and Anne ends as the failed Madame Bovary which Mme Duras had been careful not to make her. The 'expérience intérieure' is obscured rather than illuminated and, in the absence of a more elliptical and less explicit approach, the film of *Moderato cantabile* remains 'une histoire d'amour' and not, as Mme Duras insists, 'une histoire de l'amour'.

Much then has been lost in the process of transferring the novel to the screen, but much too has been gained. Set at Blaye in the Gironde, the film lacks a sea but makes the most of a moody, oily river. And if the stark black and white fails to pick out the colours which underscore Anne's search, the monochrome effect is appropriately bleak. The camera lingers on gates and railings which become a vivid metaphor for Anne's imprisonment, while the intercutting of exteriors and interiors in the dinner scene graphically conveys both her distress and her yearning. The identification of Anne with the dead woman (whose pose and scream she mimes) and of Chauvin with the murderer (at one point he grasps her roughly by the throat) is complete in a way the novel cannot match. And if the suggestive powers of colour are absent, sound comes into its own. The siren, the radio, the metronome, the click of billiard balls, the noise of the docks — all intrude insistently. Above all, Diabelli's themes provide a pointed commentary on the action.

Yet on balance the final result is an uneasy compromise between the director's sense of realism and the poetry of the book. Though the location conveyed 'parfaitement l'atmosphère qui convenait à l'histoire d'Anne Desbaresdes', Mme Duras did not find the film 'très réussi, très ressemblant au roman' (*27,* p. 68). Peter Brook was not sufficiently 'fou' to enter her idiosyncratic world and she has several times indicated that she would like to film the book herself. 'Si j'etais plus jeune, j'aurais refait *Moderato cantabile* sans script, le livre seulement. Le script fait avec Gérard Jarlot était mauvais, faux, de même la mise en scène de Peter Brook. Jarlot écrivait d'une façon très voyante, tout était à la surface de la page. De même était la mise en scène de P. Brook' (*Les Yeux Verts,* 1980, p. 31). Until such time as Mme Duras directs the film which she would have liked to see, we must be content with a version which is a stylish but adulterated comparative exercise.

Conclusion

MODERATO cantabile is a 'difficult' novel which at times seems perverse in its rejection of the conventions of fiction. We may feel that the narrator is unduly tentative and fails to deliver what appears to be promised. Instead of anecdote and a developed story line, Mme Duras gives us patterns of symbol and movement, and a tension whose origin and focus are indistinct and blurred. Yet at the same time, it is equally difficult to deny the power and the artistry of this strange and secret tale. For what we are given is a haunting and brilliantly lit study in frustration and alienation. With a remarkable depth of insight, Mme Duras weaves a subtle and fluid design which ultimately achieves the status of a poetic truth.

By any standards, *Moderato cantabile* must be regarded as a polished and accomplished work of art over which its author exerts total control. It has an air of classic purity and simplicity which disciplines the romanticism of its theme. Yet where it succeeds most, perhaps, is in *showing* a story and not in telling it. It is a 'roman de découverte' in the profoundest sense. As we follow Anne's tortured path to self-discovery, we find that the act of reading turns into another act of discovery in which we ourselves are closely implicated. For we do not so much read a story as decipher the signs and symbols and patterns which reflect the story which we are required to 'invent' for ourselves. The act of reading therefore becomes part of the novel. The murder is a 'récit absent' and Anne and Chauvin spend a great deal of time imagining the events and feelings which preceded it: they are watchers of what they have never seen. Their words and gestures are not autonomous but histrionic, for they play imagined roles. But as we observe them watching what they have not seen and remembering what they have never experienced, we become the third dimension of their 'récit absent'. It is for us to imagine, invent and ultimately recreate the drama and in so doing we make it a part of our own consciousness. Many artists count upon the support of their reader; few demand his active participation to quite such a degree.

On one level, Mme Duras seeks thus to destroy the aesthetic prejudice we may have for novels which have a beginning, a middle and an end. Indeed, she concedes that the book marks a turning point in her own writing career. For the first time she struck a note of 'laconisme' and put her 'théorie des blancs' into practice. On this aesthetic level, *Moderato cantabile* begins the process which has taken her towards more poetic forms of expression.

But her conscious wish to undermine the novel is much more than a matter of mere aesthetics. The 'destruction' she aimed for was, even in 1958, part of the wider political destruction of oppressive values of all kinds. In this sense, *Moderato* is a first draft of *Détruire, dit-elle* and Anne is a close relative of Elisabeth, the wealthy wife whose conventional certainties are cruelly, utterly but necessarily subverted. Anne may therefore be regarded as much more than an individual who stumbles towards self-knowledge, for Mme Duras has indicated that her heroine may be taken as a symbol for other forms of revolt — for feminism, for instance, or other chafings against the collective system. Love and revolution are perhaps 'impossible', but Mme Duras shows us that their pursuit can lead to the discovery and eventually to the repossession of ourselves.

A Selective Bibliography

1 (An up-to-date bibliography will be found in H. Micciolli, *Moderato Cantabile de Marguerite Duras,* Hachette, 'Collection Lire aujourd'hui', 1979.)

A. WORKS BY MME DURAS REFERRED TO IN THE TEXT

2 *La Vie tranquille* (novel), Gallimard, 1944.

3 *Un Barrage contre le Pacifique* (novel), Gallimard, 1950.

4 *Le Marin de Gibraltar* (novel), Gallimard, 1952.

5 *Les Petits Chevaux de Tarquinia* (novel), Gallimard, 1953.

6 *Des Journées entières dans les arbres* (stories: with *Le Boa, Mme Dodin* and *Les Chantiers*), Gallimard, 1954.

7 *Moderato cantabile* (novel), Les Editions de Minuit, 1958.

8 *Hiroshima mon amour* (film script), Gallimard, 1960.

9 *Les Viaducs de la Seine-et-Oise* (play), Gallimard, 1960.

10 *Dix heures et demie du soir en été* (novel), Gallimard, 1960.

11 *L'Après-midi de Monsieur Andesmas* ('récit'), Gallimard, 1962.

12 *Le Ravissement de Lol V. Stein* (novel), Gallimard, 1964.

13 *Le Vice-Consul* (novel), Gallimard, 1966.

14 *Détruire, dit-elle* (novel), Les Editions de Minuit, 1969. Also released as a feature film in 1969.

15 *Nathalie Granger, suivi de la Femme du Gange,* Gallimard, 1973 (text of two films released in 1973).

16 *India Song* ('texte, théâtre, film'), Gallimard, 1973. (Text of feature film released in 1974.)

17 *Les Parleuses* (conversations with Xavière Gauthier, May-July 1973), Les Editions de Minuit, 1974.

18 *Le Camion,* Les Editions de Minuit, 1977. (Text of feature film released in 1977.)

B. SUGGESTIONS FOR FURTHER READING

1. *General studies*

19 Cismaru, Alfred, *Marguerite Duras,* New York, Twayne Publishers Inc., 1971 (Twayne's World Authors, 147).

20 Vircondelet, Alain, *Marguerite Duras,* Seghers, 1972.

21 Seylaz, Jean-Luc, *Les romans de Marguerite Duras. Essai sur une thématique de la durée,* Archives des Lettres Modernes, no. 1, 1963.

2. *Editions of 'Moderato cantabile'*

22 *Moderato cantabile, suivi de 'L'Univers romanesque de Marguerite Duras', par Henri Hell, et du Dossier de Presse de 'Moderato cantabile',* Coll. 10/18, 1962.

23 *Moderato cantabile. Edited by W. J. Strachan,* Methuen's Twentieth Century Texts, 1968.

24 *Moderato cantabile. Edited by Thomas Bishop,* Englewood Cliffs, Prentice Hall, 1968.

25 *Moderato cantabile. Présenté et commenté par Jean Bessière,* Bordas, 1972.

3. *Interviews and articles*

26 Bishop, Lloyd, 'Classical structure and style in *Moderato cantabile', French Review,* XLVII, special issue no. 6 (Spring 1974), pp. 219-234.

27 Bourdet, Denise, *Brèves rencontres,* Grasset, 1963, pp. 65-71.

28 Bourin, André, 'Marguerite Duras' (interview), *Les Nouvelles Littéraires* (18 June 1959), pp. 1, 4.

29 Chapsal, Madeleine, *Quinze entretiens,* Julliard, 1963, pp. 55-64.

30 Kneller, J. W., 'Elective empathies and musical affinities', *Yale French Studies,* 27 (1961), pp. 114-120.

31 Knapp, Bettina, 'Interviews avec Marguerite Duras et Gabriel Cousin', *French Review,* XLIV, 4 (March 1971), pp. 653 *et seq.*

32 Sutton, Nina, 'Asking for the impossible' (interview), *The Guardian* (13 July 1971), p. 8.

33 Zepp, Evelyn H., 'Language as ritual in Marguerite Duras' *Moderato cantabile', Symposium,* XXX, 3 (Fall 1976), pp. 236-259.

34 (Anon), 'L'Auteur d'*Hiroshima mon amour* vous parle', *Réalités,* 206 (March 1963), pp. 90-95.